Administrative

Explorations

Contributors:

David Alsop
John Bloom
Bill Bottom
Agaf Dancy
Abraham Entin
Siegfried Finser
Lynn Kern
Dorothy Lenz
David Mitchell
Dana Myers
Martin Novom
Cornelis Pieterse
Louis Rossi
Christopher Schaefer
Robert Schiappacasse
Kay Skonieczny
Ann Stahl

Edited by: DAVID MITCHELL
& DAVE ALSOP

Published by:

The Association of Waldorf Schools of North America
3911 Bannister Road
Fair Oaks, CA 95628

Title: **Administrative Explorations**

Editors: David Mitchell and Dave Alsop

Proofreader: Nancy Jane

Cover: Elisabeth Auer

ISBN # 1-888365-25-0

Table of Contents

Introduction

by

David Mitchell and Dave Alsop

T he one thing we can all count upon in life is that things will change. In order to keep abreast of the changes in the financial and organizational thinking of Waldorf schools in North America, we offer you this collection of essays as an update to *Economic Explorations*, first published in 1988.

We believe that this collection of essays will bring great rewards to the reader, in the form of perspectives from which to view one's local situation. Images ranging from pillars to plant metamorphosis to center and periphery abound in addressing the overall growth and development of a Waldorf school. Practical matters from enrollment to planned giving to budget preparation are addressed in detail, offering the reader insights into the essential questions of why, how and what. Thoughts about leadership, joyful philanthropy, and achieving a spirit of determined cooperation among all members of a Waldorf school community are here, too. Truly, a living and inspiring imagination of healthy schools emerges for the reader, with a great deal of practical, down to earth advice included.

As an Association we have come a long way in the past decade. Our school movement continues to grow, and new ideas have come forth. We are grateful for the existence of DANA (the Development and Administrative Network of AWSNA), which made this revision possible through its financial support. DANA, comprised of a dedicated group of individuals in Waldorf schools all across North America, has focused attention upon many aspects of the business lives of our schools, raising the standard by which Waldorf education meets the public on a daily basis.

A companion, spiral-bound booklet, entitled *Administrative Explorations Addendum* containing examples of administrative forms, spreadsheets, and related material, can be purchased as a supplement to this volume through AWSNA Publications.

Chapter 1

Three Pillars of Healthy Waldorf School Communities – Cultivating the Parent-Teacher Partnership

by

Robert Schiappacasse

Together, parents and teachers found, develop, and sustain Waldorf schools around the world. Without this partnership we would have no Waldorf schools, just as without the spiritual insights of Anthroposophy, Waldorf education as we know it would not be possible. Over the course of the 20th century tremendous efforts have been made to establish training centers for teachers to meet the growing need for schools. At the beginning of the 21st century, the pedagogical culture of Waldorf education is rooted in our schools and training centers in North America. Although more teachers are continually needed, our pedagogical work is established and moving out of the pioneer phase of its development. However, our ability to build more conscious and effective partnerships between teachers and parents is still very much in its infancy and needs further support and development. If Waldorf education is to more firmly root itself in our communities in the 21st century, a more explicit partnership culture needs to be developed that helps our schools grow as communities of body, soul, and spirit. Rudolf Steiner once indicated that it would be a "tragedy if the social impulse that is the foundation of the Waldorf school were ignored." How parents and teachers work together is one of the foundations of the social impulse which allows our schools to grow and develop. How can the same level of expertise and effectiveness that many teachers achieve in creating the classroom community be cultivated and achieved in the building of the Waldorf school community as a whole?

The essential roles of parents and teachers in creating and developing Waldorf schools can be summarized in the following way: Teachers have the responsibility to guide the incarnation of the child, and parents have the responsibility to incarnate the school. Clearly, without teaching expertise a healthy classroom community can not be formed and sustained. If the teaching in the classroom is not adequate, the core of the school's existence is endangered. Likewise, if the partnership with parents is not alive and effective in a way that parents experience themselves as stakeholders and carriers of the school's development, then the social and financial vitality, indeed, the very existence of the school, is at risk. Without the expertise, participation, and financial support of parents, the school itself, as a home for Waldorf education, cannot achieve its stability and maturity in the wider community. Together, parents and teachers create the social climate and the physical environment in which the soul of the school becomes visible.

It is my experience that two distinctive kinds of talent are needed to develop a healthy classroom culture and a school community as a whole. It is helpful to acknowledge from the outset that the capacities and talents necessary to be effective in these two different spheres are, in many ways, diametrically opposite. A picture of these two distinctive capacities or talents can be found in the Biblical stories of the Old Testament, in the lineage of Cain and Abel.

Abel was a keeper of sheep, and Cain was a tiller of the land. Their differences are well known, and Cain's murder of his brother led him, by God's command, to wander the earth. His offspring include Tubal-Cain, who was the forger of all instruments of bronze and iron. Cain's lineage seeks to master the practical realm. Abel's death led to the birth of Seth who was ordained by God to carry forward the lineage of Abel and his earnest fidelity to the divine world. Out of Seth's line came Solomon, who was endowed with great wisdom. Of this Rudolf Steiner said, "This wisdom can be expressed in words which go straight to the human heart and can uplift a person, but it is unable to produce anything tangible of a technical nature, in art and science." From the line of Cain are born the creators of art and science, those who can penetrate the secrets of earthly life. One of these was Hiram, who was a contemporary of Solomon. When Solomon decides to build a temple to embody his great wisdom, he seeks out Hiram who has the worldly skills to build it. In this story we are presented with a picture having deep meaning. The very foundations of earthly culture require those, who like Solomon, are in possession of divine wisdom, and those like Hiram who are skillful and resourceful, knowing how to shape and form earthly matter out of their willful resolve. Enmity arises between these two when the Queen of Sheba comes seeking Solomon and his wisdom, and then becomes smitten by one glance of the powerful presence of Hiram. The Queen of Sheba, a picture of the soul of humanity, is in love with both. A partnership which unites both soul capacities is necessary to manifest Solomon's temple.

To explore the many levels of meaning in this story would take us too far afield. We can sense, however, that this is a story which makes visible a powerful soul-polarity that weaves through history. It demonstrates dramatically how the manifestation of significant contributions to human culture require the co-working of individuals with strikingly different talents. The dynamic polarity portrayed in the relationship of Solomon and Hiram stands archetypally at the root of human culture, and at the root of the development of Waldorf schools. Rudolf Steiner gave many lectures at the end of his life stressing the need for these two streams to unite at the end of the 20th century and contribute an important spiritual impulse to the soul culture of the 21st century. Our task is to awaken to this dynamic polarity which is alive in our communities, and make it culturally productive through a more conscious partnership that recognizes and appreciates the varied human capacities which create and embody our Waldorf school communities.

In our Waldorf communities we can see how the teachers work to cultivate a wise relationship to the developing child. Their role is a priestly one. They seek to bring the right influences to the children in the classroom, at the right time, to foster their healthy incarnation. At the same time they must cultivate individually, and together with colleagues, a deepening relationship to the spiritual foundations of their work. Through preparation, observation, study, and inner development, their work with the children becomes living and fruitful. Parents, on the other hand, provide most of the resources which allow our Waldorf schools to come into being and grow. As well, they bring a wide range of skills and experience which the school needs for its development. Without their participation and practical expertise in business, finance, real estate, publicity, management, administration, architecture, construction, fundraising, and much else, our schools could not grow and develop in the world.

We can see at a glance that these two soul streams are at work in helping to realize the goals of Waldorf education and the building of Waldorf schools around the world. It is also evident that the relationship between these two soul streams in our schools is not always harmonious.

Waldorf ideals can not always be fully embraced by parents, especially those new to the school. And, the practical support for the education will not just "materialize" without skill and effort. Without a shared vision between the "teacher-priests" and the "school builders," like the co-working of Solomon and Hiram, the temple of Waldorf education can not be realized in a way that makes our schools life-imbued, harmonious, and strong.

In order for our Waldorf schools to be healthy, teachers and parents need to share the responsibility for creating, sustaining, and embodying their life and culture. Rudolf Steiner indicated the new direction that we must take to create a healthy Waldorf culture early in the century in his writings on the threefold social organism. He wisely outlined how human society and organizations need to seek a threefold organization, which lives archetypally in the human form and physiognomy. The metabolic system, nerve-sense system, and heart-lung rhythmic systems of the body interpenetrate and wisely cooperate when the body is healthy. Similarly, the social order that human beings freely create needs to reflect this wise threefold ordering of head, heart, and limb in a way that the common good is served and the whole is balanced and healthy. I believe that Steiner's indications make it clear that our communities need to be cooperatively based rather than hierarchical in character. By identifying the threefold nature of our schools, the 1) spiritual/cultural, 2) social and interpersonal, and 3) economic, we can begin to recognize in broad outlines the three spheres which need to be identified and cultivated appropriately for the good of the whole. The following illustration can help us identify the "three pillars of Waldorf school culture."

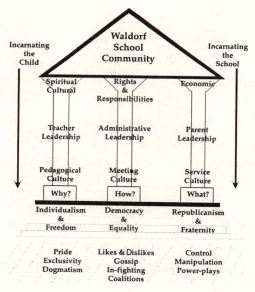

I have drawn an arrow on the left and right side of this diagram to indicate the fundamental polarity between teachers and parents which I spoke to above. On the left side stands the "spiritual/cultural pillar," and to the left of it the arrow indicating the role of the teachers to take primary responsibility for the incarnation of the child. The spiritual/cultural pillar, next to this arrow, represents the spiritual foundation of the pedagogy and its practice which creates a pedagogical culture in the school. This is a realm of individualism and freedom without which the insights needed to educate would not be forthcoming. At the pillar's base is the question "Why," indicating the striving to understand and acquire practical pedagogical insight. Here the teacher is the king or queen of their classroom, and faculty meetings are a learning community led by those who are most capable. When this pole is taken to its extreme, it becomes "Luciferic," tending toward dogmatism, pride, and exclusivity. The right goal of this sphere is individuality and insight.

On the right side of the diagram is an arrow representing a realm where the expertise and leadership of parents is primary. This represents the "incarnation of the school." Next to this arrow stands the "economic pillar" characterizing the work-life or service-culture of the school. This sphere's health is safeguarded by the principle of "republicanism," or the maxim that those who are the most capable in a particular realm should be entrusted with the work. Ideally it is a realm of practicality, professionalism, and competency. Here lives the ethic, "What can I do for you?" At the base of this pillar is the question "What," to identify the concrete tasks which serve to embody the school in the community. When this pole is taken to a negative extreme, it becomes "Ahrimanic," and can be characterized by attempts to control, power-plays, and manipulation. The higher goal of this sphere is efficiency and service.

In Waldorf school culture, our greatest strength, a teacher-centric foundation, so beneficial to the creation of the classroom culture, can be our greatest weakness when we attempt to cultivate economic health and stability. The economic spheres of our schools are often hampered by misunderstandings, such as the notion suggesting that Waldorf schools are "teacher-run schools." It is precisely in the economic realm, where a parent-based Board of Trustees, in association with core faculty, needs to take primary responsibility and leadership. Here, the expertise of parents is most needed to embody the school through the leadership of those who are most resourceful in the school community. These two realms are often, of necessity, at odds with each other. In seeking to bring balance to these two outer pillars of Waldorf culture, we need to consider the pillar that stands between them.

At the center of our diagram stands the pillar which represents the interpersonal or relational life of our school. Here the "rights and responsibilities" of all who are participants in the life of the school need to be overseen and cultivated. At its base is the question "How," indicating that this central pillar oversees the articulation, cultivation, and maintenance of the processes by which we work together in our schools. This is in particular the realm where the administration of the school is active. This middle pillar represents the "meeting culture" of the school, and is characterized by the striving for shared participation, fairness, and equality. The administration, and its leadership in a school, may include both parents and teachers, selected for their competence. Here must live the ethic of inclusiveness and cooperation which requires a transparency and clarity in how agreements are reached, decisions made, conflicts addressed, decisions are being carried out, as well as how a dialogue of understanding is cultivated and sustained between individuals and throughout the bodies of the school. This sphere in its negative extreme can become plagued by social unrest and chaos caused by unchecked gossip, a social climate dominated by likes, dislikes, distrust, and suspicion, resulting in coalitions and factions. The appropriate goal of this sphere is cooperation and partnership.

Like the threefold human body, our schools are healthy when a dynamic balance can be maintained between each of the three realms. When one pillar in our Waldorf school is weak, or dominates the others, the school is weakened. The more these three spheres can be empowered with explicit leadership, competency, clear expectations and communication procedures, the more support each area can give to the others and the less likely will be the tendency to polarization.

The middle pillar of our schools is often the most overlooked and misunderstood. When it is not strong, the parent-teacher partnership will be hampered. A weakness here often stems from our historic mistrust of administration due to a mis-reading of Steiner writings. His comments about administration are largely leveled at the public school system of his time and its control by the state. Steiner wanted the educational process to be free from state control and teachers to be free from restrictive administrators entering into the pedagogical affairs of the classroom. He wanted teachers to "have a hand in the entire administration and business life of the school...," not to dominate it inappropriately. When we cultivate the middle pillar in a way that is supportive of Waldorf culture and values, and through a vocationally based administration, with clearly defined administrative roles, responsibilities, and practices, a spirit of inclusiveness and partnership can suffuse our schools. However, to create this climate in a way that opens the door to greater participation, several persistent misconceptions need to be overcome.

First, we need to open ourselves to the viewpoint that the spirit of the school does not only inform the life of the school through the College of Teachers, or the Faculty Council. We need to observe how the spirit of the school can be present "wherever two or more are gathered," at work on behalf of the school community. This can take place in the classroom through the work of the teacher, and in the social and work life of the school where parents and teachers are active. When we experience how this spirit works throughout the life of the community, we are freed from a certain mental bondage which can limit our ability to appreciate how others in our midst can be full partners in the work of the school.

Second, we must recognize that what potentially makes our schools unique is that they are self-administered, rather than teacher-run. The latter implies that teachers in all cases have the necessary experience to lead in all three spheres of the school, which is generally not the case. It is, of course, central to the first pillar of Waldorf culture that the schools have a faculty directed pedagogy. In the words of Stockmeyer, a close associate of Steiner in the first Waldorf School, "The school's curriculum and internal workings, including the method of teaching, (shall) be handled within, by the teachers." Stockmeyer clearly identifies Steiner's wishes for parent participation when he noted, "parents . . . would have access to the school's business and administration." This understanding, which is also very much my experience in Waldorf schools, welcomes parents to enter into responsible roles in the life of the school community.

Third, administration in the consensus climate of a Waldorf school does not mean making decisions over the heads of the teachers. To more fully incarnate the middle pillar of our schools we need to transform our fear of administration as "control" to an expectation of an administration whose goal is service and servant leadership. If administrators share the spiritual foundations that inform the work of the teacher, they can work together to develop and maintain the agreements which give order and clarity to the procedural life of the school. A correct understanding of the three spheres of the school and their interworking on behalf of the spiritual/pedagogical goals of Waldorf education will preclude any interfering with the pedagogical leadership of the teachers.

Finally, it must be recognized that core administrative work and administrative leadership require capacities that are very different from those required in the classroom. All teachers can contribute more or less to the administrative life of the school, but the larger a school becomes, the more leadership in this middle realm must be in the hands of individuals who have the experience and special capacities that are required. These include strong written and verbal communications skills, an understanding for and love of the process or procedure essential to resolving questions that come to light, good interpersonal abilities, group facilitation and conflict resolution skills, as well as skillfulness in meeting facilitation and the methods of consensus decision making.

Our teachers are expected to complete Waldorf teacher training programs. Shouldn't there be a comparable training in Waldorf Administration? We need to develop professional training for Waldorf administration and support and encourage capable individuals who have found their way into our school communities to pursue them. These trainings and programs can incorporate anthroposophical "Foundation Year" studies, and an overview of the stages of child development with training in the threefold social organism, Waldorf school administration, the stages of school development, and the art of community development.

Our schools need capable, committed and trained administrative co-workers who are full-partners in the life of our schools. When alongside Waldorf teachers trained in child development we can develop trained administrative co-workers, the middle pillar of Waldorf school culture will be better able to support the cooperation and co-working of parents and teachers in our schools.

Identifying the three pillars upon which our Waldorf culture develops can also help us to move from a volunteer culture to a leadership culture in each of the three spheres. Too often we mistakenly allow the consensus culture of Waldorf schools to disable initiative and leadership in all three spheres of the school. We need to more consciously cultivate pedagogical leadership, administrative leadership, and Board and Parent Council leadership by identifying individuals based on competence, and giving them and committees clear mandates and job descriptions on behalf of those they serve. Waldorf schools are not served by the "top-down" leadership of corporate culture. They require leadership of a new kind that is based on demonstrated capacities, trust in partnership, confidence in dialogue and the process of consensus building, and the ideal of servant leadership. Individuals with these qualifications who are identified and clearly mandated can serve the three spheres of the school by coordinating the work of the whole. Through regular meetings the workings of the school are overviewed, prioritized, coordinated, and furthered. The more we empower, cultivate, and support a culture of leadership throughout the three spheres of our schools, one which more consciously includes the parent-teacher partnership underlying our schools, the more the good spirit of Waldorf education will be enabled to work in our midst.

As we move into the 21st century, we have a tremendous opportunity in Waldorf school communities to further incarnate the social impulse in Waldorf education through how we learn to work together in our adult community of teachers and parents. We are drawn together through the children to form destiny communities which will further the incarnation of their germinating capacities. Perhaps what Hillary Clinton suggested in her recent book is true, if in a slightly different sense. It does take a whole village to educate a child. What is distinctive about our Waldorf "villages" is that they are created and built by teachers who are free to teach, and parents who are skillful and resourceful, working together toward a common goal. Like Solomon and Hiram, we are drawn together by destiny to offer divergent talents and resources to make manifest unique cultural centers dedicated to the developing human being and a more truly human culture. A clearer understanding of the three pillars of a Waldorf school community, and the parent-teacher partnership underlying its realization, can help us to more consciously incarnate the social impulse in our developing Waldorf school communities.

Chapter 2

Form and Flux: Some Observations on the Organization of a Waldorf School

by

John Bloom

It is my hope that this article makes visible the forms, functions, and formative capacities of all of the organizational elements at work in a Waldorf school. Further, my intention is to portray a school not just as educating children, but also as spiritually soul-nourished and nourishing for all the rest of those who participate in and contribute to its life. For a school to serve its public cultural mission it must fully understand itself as a social entity, and ideally each individual should feel a connection to and place within that entity. I would like to approach this organizational understanding from the perspectives of its forms (its governing bodies and structures, how those bodies evolve over time) and the powers of social ideals and intentions. I think it is fair to say at the outset that striving and failure are a constant in reconciling intention and ideal with reality.

To begin with, let's start with groups—namely, the Faculty, College of Teachers, Board of Trustees, Board committees, and Parents Association and its committees, and the Administration. There is nothing unusual in this list, and every Waldorf school has groups that fulfill these roles, though they may use different names. Hopefully, each of these groups holds the children and their needs at the center and finds its appropriate form for meetings and social working to best accomplish its tasks in serving the school.

The primary form of a school is its corporate status (usually a not-for-profit charitable status as determined by the state). The corporation, the physical body of the school, is usually entrusted to the Board of Trustees, who in many ways are actually serving the public. The school, from one perspective, then incarnates within the corporation, or, from another perspective, operates under the aegis of the corporation. In either case, it is important to note that the corporation and the school are not the same forms, though, of course, neither would exist without the other. Interestingly enough, the parents are connected to the corporation by membership and economics, and to the school through its cultural service, the education it provides their children. They pay tuition to the corporation and send their children to school!

To the imagination of each of these forms, one now has to add its flux, its process of change over time. One can observe that each of the groups is in a constant state of transformation, though each of the transformations has a different character and happens at a different rate. Board of Trustees members have terms of office so that change is planned into the structure— one might call this a term of service. The teachers, provided everything runs smoothly, have a much longer tenure, sometimes a lifetime—a term of devotion. Parents actually grow into the school over time while their children attend. This coming to terms with the school one could call a kind of communion.

Service, devotion, and communion have distinct yet integrally related qualities, and each contributes to a vital community. Of course, aspects of all three live in each of the bodies, yet the inner gesture of each contributes something particular to the working of the social life of the school. In developing an understanding of these contributions, the deep values held by all of the working community members should become visible. The degree to which these values are shared (and it is amazing how frequently, given the time needed to understand each other's language and intentions, that there is a profound accord) conditions an organization's capacity for community development. Articulation and resonation of shared values foster inclusion by all those participating in the school and are powerful tools for reaching out to find friends (including grandparents) in the wider community.

To evolve and maintain a healthy school, each of the participatory bodies needs to develop and enable a capacity for change for itself and for each other. As each considers its own evolutionary form—this is what is meant by "self-perpetuating" (Board), "teacher-guided" (Faculty), and "association" (Parents)—a sense of the past and the seeds of the future must live in every assessment of the present. This is a very subtle task, because it means that each of the bodies needs to be nourished and needs to nourish each other by a common source. It also means that though each of the bodies has special tasks, each must be constantly developing a sense of the whole, the grander form. Understanding this concept, as well as the notion that a shared sense of planning and vision is the binding force in a school community, is key to the mandate of trust which each of the organs needs from the others in order to do its service.

To the form and its flux one can add multiple contemporaneous imaginations of it. One could say that the grander form (but not the essence) of the school changes depending upon which organ is meeting and imagining it at any given time. Each group has its lens, language, and consciousness, its metaphors and frames of reference, its intentions and its purpose. These elements inevitably condition a group's perception and place it in a particular relation to the whole. As a group works together over time, it develops a being or character which in turn, for better or worse, has the capacity to inform, at one level, and to govern at another, the group's work. The group's being should be recognized as inseparable from the school's formative process, its form, its being, and worked with accordingly. This approach to and quality of work require some grounding in spiritual intention and a capacity for objective yet participatory perception.

In the late eighteenth century, Johann Wolfgang von Goethe published his research on metamorphosis as a guiding principle in nature, particularly with respect to plants. One of the most intriguing aspects of this principle is the idea that in the developing plant each part, though different in appearance and function, is a metamorphosis of the part to which it is connected in sequence and from which it evolved. What we do not necessarily see but must know is that the etheric or life force is the sculptor in this unfolding process. Each of the parts owes its existence and form to its predecessor, though its function may be quite different. Goethe further looked to the principle of expansion and contraction as a principle of metamorphosis. Within each seed is the possibility of the whole plant, but it lies there in a condensed, contracted form. The seed expands through root and leaf, contracts into the calyx wherein the future seeds form through the pollination process of the flowering expansion. Goethe was able to perceive the seed in the form of the leaf; he was in a sense mapping a divine intention. Though we may not be able to see what Goethe saw, we know that it is certainly there by possibility. Driven by both inner imperative and outer necessity, the growth process engenders parts that are functionally harmonious: Systemic logic would have all parts integrated through morphogenic principle. In such an integral system over time, the dysfunction of any part has consequences for the whole organism and its capacity for renewal.

The poetic of such an image can illuminate our thinking regarding the development of our schools. In the expanding and contracting of the developing organism, the spatial and temporal are central. The spatial aspect is the expansion and contraction of form. The temporal is the growth and decay, with germination through the seed the link between past and future. Our culture has conditioned us to prize expansion and growth while seeing contraction and decay as negative—clearly a condition that needs rectifying if one is to work without prejudice in a developing initiative and to be awake to what lives to unfold in the future.

To see the College of Teachers as a morphogenesis of the Board of Trustees is an interesting challenge. The Board carries and forms the corporate entity which, like our own bodies, becomes the physical and fiscal reality within which the school is given its possibility. Thus, one of its first tasks in addition to finding a home site is to find a teacher or teachers who can transform this possibility into a reality—the educational process which is based upon the communication of wisdom in the form of capacities. As the faculty grows, one of its goals is often the formation of a College of Teachers which, by its commitment to Anthroposophy and to the development of the school, consciously connects to the spiritual impulse guiding the school. By all appearances, the Board and College, which at best work on systemic advice and consent, mutual trust, and common understanding of mission, and at worst on sporadic communication and adversarial distrust, are quite different in function and composition. But in the formation and development of most Waldorf schools, the Board of Trustees precedes the College of Teachers, often by many years, and in the formative stages carries with the few teachers the responsibility for the school's pedagogical and spiritual impulses. With the forming of a faculty and founding of a College of Teachers, these latter two impulses primarily become its purview. Regardless of the circumstances surrounding this mitotic moment, both the Board and College tend to become so busy with their respective tasks that the spiritual-morphogenic connection fades in the differentiation. It is rare and unwise for a College to divorce itself from the legal and financial aspects of the school; it is also equally important for the Board to continue to recognize the spiritual dimension of its work, especially as it gains in fiduciary, financial, and legal expertise. It may be that a harmoniously working Board is fulfilling its spiritual task, particularly if it consciously and freely serves the school's cultural mission. Would some kind of meditative work be appropriate for a Board? Shouldn't some of the College members, for example, delve deeply into the realm of finances from an anthroposophical perspective out of interest, capacity, and a willingness to engage in dialogue with Trustees? Though some of the Trustees may be less familiar with threefold economic concepts than faculty, the Trustees are often pragmatically attuned to the economic life of the world. And, are faculty members reporting on school life at the Board and Parent Association such that the spiritual striving that lives within the classroom becomes palpable and practical?

The curriculum and the profound knowledge of child development that lie behind it are based upon an active conscious acknowledgment of a spiritual reality. In essence, the teacher perceives and works with each child as a reincarnating spirit and soul. The role of teaching then is not solely one of conveying information but rather much more about developing each child's capacities. The subtlety of this distinction and the hierarchy in what is stressed in the attendant teaching approach are a challenge to communicate, because the education's true results, as with the growing plant, become visible over extended time and through periods of expansion and contraction. The language used to speak about capacities is different from traditional academic evaluation, because it takes into account a comprehensive view of a child's incarnation. This language is often laced with unfamiliar terminology. Consequently, the bridge of understanding between teachers and parents is difficult to build, and difficult to maintain, because the children continue to grow and change.

Sometimes lost in this translation of perceptions and linguistic difficulty is a common intent—serving the children. If a parent has chosen to apply to a Waldorf school and the child is enrolled, the task is for all the adults around the child to recognize the child's needs and to work in partnership to understand what each child is calling forth as issues for the adults to address. But, it also seems that parents come to the school with needs of their own—perhaps a searching life question, perhaps a wish to merge their own expectations with the aspects of the school that seemed attractive to them. In a way, the children are also bringing us, the parents, as part of the spiritual mosaic of the school. This kind of partnership is in reality a shared mission and requires that teachers and parents find a new way of working together which demands more than anything else a profound openness and ability for elevated listening— listening through the words to intent—and speaking which makes the speaker's ideals apparent. This is no simple task, but is really the basis for forming long-term teacher-parent relationships which ultimately support the children's experience.

In trying to find their place in the school, parents often meet the question of power and authority and how it works, or who has it in a Waldorf school. These questions are actively worked with by the College and the Trustees. At least, the Trustees and College know that the responsibility, authority, and power rightly belong under this heading— for the school and corporation lie within their collective or collaborative actions. Parents, on the other hand, tend to experience a distance from the decision-making processes, a distance that can sometimes produce frustration and confusion. Overcoming this distance and aligning the divergent interests of the parents with the mission of the school define the task of the Parent Association. In many ways the parents are transpirators: They breathe the world into the school and the school into the world. Enrollment (expansion and the basis for transformation) has historically been most effective by word of mouth (and the word is carried on the breath). Schools are often so busy with their internal processes that they forget or do not have resources to pay attention to what transpires from the parents, unless there is a funding campaign, or some crisis brings focus. Community-based planning, a forum for casual and ongoing conversations, is a healthy way for a school to check in on the "transpirators." Such a process can be informative and preventive in many ways.

Administration serves the common intention of the institution and is a transparent binding or facilitating entity. Of course, a school serves first the needs of the children. In a sense they have called the teachers to lead them even as in their becoming they make clear their physical, soul, and spiritual needs. This quality of servant leadership aptly describes the role of the administrators as well, but they serve the community rather than an individual pupil or class. And it is a misunderstood position since it is not a position of power in the sense of the traditional head of school. It is instead a position of service to Board and Faculty, to support and free them to fulfill their tasks and responsibilities. Yet, the administrator is often the spokesperson for the school, its most public representative, and is responsible for making sure the school is run fiscally and physically effectively.

The administrator's primary instruments for gauging the developmental state of a school are the operating budget and balance sheets. The life of the school should be visible through it in much the same way that we come to know the students through their work. Each of the financial documents has a different relationship to time. The operating budget is quite literally day to day, month to month. It establishes normative functions, and it tracks expectations, assumptions, and intentions at the beginning of the fiscal year as they transform into performance during and reflection at the end of the year. It is a wonderful exercise to work backwards through a budget year to remember the adjustments and degree of consciousness and intuition that played into the delicately interrelated elements of the school's economy. The expected and the unexpected in income and expenses are a clue to the presence of the school's being at work in the economic realm.

It is the responsibility of the administration in conjunction with the College of Teachers to carry the school's biography in depth with the knowledge that whatever qualities live in the school will have a corresponding quantitative reflection, and visa-versa. This linkage can sometimes be painful—drops in enrollment are a case in point—but it can also be useful in leading to a common understanding of the state of the school among the College, Board, and Parents. Income and expense represent values, priorities, educational goals, the well-being of those who work in the community, and the support (financial and moral) of the parents that makes the education possible through tuition and contributions.

Balancing a budget is really a misleading term. As a metaphor it implies a bilateral scale, and as such cannot encompass the full dimension of a school's operations. The picture, to be more useful, needs to be more plastic, more awake to the human realities that live behind the numbers, more attuned to the subtleties of cause and effect, direct and indirect. It is the administrator's responsibility to carry this imagination of the whole, to be able to articulate, even if intuitively rather than mathematically, how any program-related decision or financial transaction will affect the whole of the school's operation from the present into the future.

The balance sheet is a cumulative or historical record of the school's finances in the fund balance, its property value or equity, its earthly possessions like desks and chairs, and any restricted or unrestricted endowment. It is, in a sense, a measure of the physical or material aspect of money, because it constitutes the school's net worth, its value in real dollars, were the school to cease operations. This has the feel of the physical body devoid of its formative forces. The balance sheet harbors no intentions, no vision, though it certainly figures, along with the capacity to generate free gifts, into the financial thinking about what is possible. Like the calyx of the plant, it is a vessel for the seeds.

One need only turn to the realm of money to see the community's values reflected. For the Faculty, money's role is to make it possible to teach the children with all its necessary spiritual and material manifestations. For the Board, money represents the essential quantitative view of the quality of the school's operations and capacity for growth. For the parents, money represents purchase and choice in offering their children an education. It is remarkable when one assesses what this looks like in terms of intention; it almost feels like three intentions at cross purposes—almost. Let's revisit the three bodies. Money allows the teachers to be free of material concerns to focus on the spiritual-cultural tasks of teaching—one kind of freedom. Board members volunteer their services to the school based on expertise, and in volunteering define a second form of freedom—free association. Parents, given the financial resources, application and acceptance, choose one particular school from a palette of choices—a third form of freedom, selection. Within the intentions borne by these three forms of freedom, there is a critical and powerful interdependence. Freedom is necessary in order to create the necessity of freedom (chicken/egg?). In this moral entanglement lives a binding spiritual principle. The freedom each of the bodies needs comes with a concomitant sacrifice—that of giving up one's lower self-serving ego for the purpose of serving the school, informed by the spiritual guidance of the school's being. There needs to be as much clarity and consciousness about the sacrifice and the discipline it takes to make it fruitful as there is about the freedom.

Perhaps the spiritual ideal of the school can be articulated as follows—that the community of teachers, parents, and trustees places itself at the service of the children. The spiritual reality is that the community's impulses and intentions in striving toward the future are sensed by the children, become a part of them, and inspire them. The shadow side of this imagination of the ideal has to be acknowledged and guarded against: that the teachers' primary motivation is to earn money; that the Board rescinds its mandate to the teachers and assumes responsibility for the curriculum and the running of the school; that parents wield their tuition dollars as power to allow the school to exist or not depending on whether it conforms to their expectations. Were these conditions to occur, the school would experience its counter-ideal. That which aimed for freedom would instead be about power and control; cooperation turns to confrontation. As with the morphogenic principle in

20

plant development, the consequences to the development of the school and children would be devastating.

This example points directly back to the axiom: Form follows intention. And intention in the sociopolitical sphere is fairly easily grasped since it is deeply ingrained as a value structure in the Western mind set—a person (or organization) is presumed to intend the natural consequences of his, her, or its actions. Our codes of conduct and behavior from the kindergarten classroom to the workplace are based on this concept. We also tend to apply it in the economic sphere as well. Look at how we handle the nature of risk in investments. However, intention in the economic realm needs to be reexamined if a school community is to reckon with its most visible, conceptual, and volatile arena, namely, money. If we can take the idea of transformation as a central and necessary part of the operational imagination of the life of the school, then it is possible to construe tuition as an offering in support of freedom for the educational process rather than as purchase or investment with an expectation for return. The spiritual deed in the economic sphere is the greater, the lesser the degree that intention is conditional. And it should be noted that our culture has conditioned us to attach expectations of power to our dollars—the phrase "purchase power" could not be more apt.

One can begin to see how the organizational form and flux of a school determine its beauty and practicality, by coming to know the intentions and responsibilities of its constituent bodies and of the individuals who make up those bodies. This is quite some work, and it needs to be done by each of the individuals, including all the parents. One cannot know another's intention until it is spoken, or until it is inferred from an action. However, knowing by inference is a kind of belated consciousness which serves, through presumption, the legal realm well, but the cultural realm poorly. For a school to function well, intentions need to be spoken and known in an ongoing, forthright, freedom-centered trialogue. It is an administrative responsibility to ensure that appropriate forums and opportunities are provided to support that trialogue. Out of articulating and working toward the school's ideals, each of its carrying members links with the being of the school, is in turn guided by it, and is challenged to meet each other in community in a new way. It should be recognized that striving and failure are a constant in reconciling intention and ideal with reality. This notion is integral to the character of freedom and necessary for the growth of a healthy Waldorf school.

See Johann Wolfgang von Goethe, *The Metamorphosis of Plants*, Bio-Dynamic Literature: Wyoming (RI), 1978, with an introduction by Rudolf Steiner for an in-depth discussion.

Chapter 3

Phases of Waldorf School Development

by

Chris Schaefer, PhD.

A problem of our time is not knowing that there are principles for building social and societal forces as binding as the laws of mechanics.[1]
- Rudolf Steiner

The following description of school development gives a general picture of characteristic phases in the life cycle of a Waldorf school.[2] It is meant to provide a perspective or guide to aid faculty, administration, parents, and Board members to more consciously develop their school. The picture presented in no way seeks to deny the uniqueness of each Waldorf school's biography, but rather to point toward characteristic questions and issues which exist in the life history of most schools.[3]

Underlying this description of the life cycle of Waldorf schools are a number of principles. The first is that all institutions are human creations; they are created by people with an idea in response to a perceived need. In the case of Waldorf schools this need is a sense that the children in a given community or region want Waldorf education. The second principle is that schools, and indeed all organizations, are living entities, with phases of adaptation, growth, crises, and development.[4] This means that organic metaphors such as seed, stalk, bud, and flower, or birth, childhood, adulthood, and old age are more relevant to the biography of schools than mechanical images such as that of an input-output system, a clockwork mechanism, or a well-running engine. In creating a school we are indeed creating a living being, whose destiny may be unknown to us, but which requires our love and ongoing commitment to flourish.

A third principle, and one which I find to be crucial, is that there is no one right form for all Waldorf schools. There are, of course, relevant principles in forming a Waldorf school, such as the idea of a collegial institution or that of phases in the life cycle of a school, but, ultimately, each group of teachers, parents, children and friends must evolve those particular forms which can most effectively express their intentions. A consequence of this principle is that school forms need to evolve and change over time in order to reflect new human and spiritual aspirations.

Working with these principles leads to a presentation of characteristic issues and developmental questions rather than specific answers. Questions bring consciousness, and consciousness is that which determines the social forms we create and how well we work within them.

Birth and Childhood: Improvising in Response to Needs

The birth of a Waldorf school has its origins in the deep commitment of one or more individuals to the ideals of Waldorf education. Such a commitment may arise through visiting an existing school, or by reading a book on Waldorf education, or through hearing an inspiring lecture. The ideals of the education light up, and an individual or a small group may say, "This community needs a Waldorf school, and I am going to work on it!" This lighting up, this moment of conception, happens in a great variety of ways. It is always interesting to go back in a school's history and find out who first conceived the imagination of the school and under what circumstances it arose. One founding personality read Rudolf Steiner's name in a book while on a plane. He then ordered many of Rudolf Steiner's lectures and was struck by those given to teachers and so resolved to start a school for English children in the U.S. in the middle of World War II. This school later became the Kimberton Waldorf School. In another quite common circumstance, a group of potential parents met at a presentation on Waldorf education; began to study A.C. Harwood's book, *The Recovery of Man in Childhood*, and decided to start a school.[5] Another common founding experience is when a trained Waldorf teacher moves to a community and resolves to start a school, as was the case with the Pine Hill Waldorf School in Wilton, New Hampshire.

Following the moment of conception is a period of gestation or pregnancy in which one or more individuals are walking around carrying an idea. This gestation period varies in time. The Toronto Waldorf School had a long preparation period; other school groups begin a kindergarten after only one or two years of preparation. During this preparation time, lectures and workshops are organized, fairs are given and the world is being told about the initiative, about the child one hopes to bring into the world. It is at times a frightening process involving many inner and outer questions. Important questions to consider are:

> Who is really committed to the school?
> What is our understanding of Waldorf education and of
>   Anthroposophy?
> How much money will we need?
> What are the right legal forms?
> Do we create a Waldorf School Association as a non-
>   profit organization?
> How do we find an experienced or a trained Waldorf
>   teacher?
> How will we know when to start?
> Where will the school be located?

These and other questions need conscious attention before the kindergarten or school opens its doors. A central issue is whether one has the intention of developing a kindergarten and a grade school or just a kindergarten. Developing a kindergarten and a grade school together or in a short sequence has many advantages, but requires a deeper and more sustaining commitment. Equally important are the questions of motive. Does the initiative group consist mainly of parents who want the school for their own children? What happens when the school or kindergarten takes a year or two longer to develop than anticipated? A core group of people whose commitment goes beyond their immediate, personal interest is essential.

Another issue is whether there is enough actual or anticipated support. Are there enough children to begin with grade one and add another grade each year? Does the region have a population adequate to support a school?

In working with very young schools or with school initiative groups, I have found seven question areas developed by my colleague Tino Voors to be most helpful. They provide a kind of check list for clarification which can help new school groups or other new initiatives avoid many of the difficulties which new ventures face in the first few years of their existence.

New school groups are usually stronger in certain areas than in others. One group has a strong sense for public relations, another for building community, a third a good sense of financial and administrative clarity. Bringing both strengths and weaknesses to consciousness early on can be a real help.

Quite a few years ago I was visiting a new school which had started ambitiously with a kindergarten and a number of grades at the same time. It was a warm afternoon, and some new faculty and Board members were discussing the next school year. It seemed to me that both enrollment and income projections were very optimistic. When a new faculty member asked whether they could rely on being paid on the first of every month, he was assured that everything would work out. I wasn't so sure, thinking that here there was much enthusiasm and hope, but limited experience with the struggle to make the finances work. In the following year my concern became a reality as the school cut salaries and dropped some grades.

Following the gestation period is the exciting moment of birth when the school or kindergarten opens its door and the children arrive for the first time. This is a very important moment in the biography of all institutions and should be celebrated accordingly. A foundation ceremony or a birthday celebration, in which teachers, parents, children, friends and visitors can participate, should be planned. In this way one invites both the visible and the invisible world to bless and support that which has been inaugurated.

If the new school flourishes, it enters a period analogous to childhood—vibrant, exciting, and, of course, full of surprises. It is a time of ups and downs, of mood swings and crises. "Will we have enough money to meet payroll?" Yet, it is also a time of blessing, of unforeseen help. I remember sitting with other parents at a new school in the Boston area that was to become the Waldorf School in Lexington, wondering about how we could cover the next month's payroll, when an anonymous donation of $2,000 arrived.

Generally, people have a high level of motivation and much warmth toward the fledgling school, because they are participating in a marvelous creation process. First, there was an idea carried by a few people—without children, teachers, money and building. To see one's dream gradually begin to incarnate is a wonderful, if also a tiring, experience.

As the new school grows, it manifests a *number of characteristic qualities,* which it shares with other new initiatives.

- It is generally of small to medium size—a kindergarten and a few grades, or perhaps even up to grade six.

- It has a shallow, informal organizational form with a limited hierarchy. Perhaps there are three sets of founding couples and two founding teachers who jointly make important decisions over a kitchen table or in a church basement.

- Leadership in the school is personal, direct and informal. New teachers and new parents may take some time to fit in, because there is a personal style of doing things. If one doesn't like this style or the personalities of those in the carrying group, social difficulties frequently follow.

- Decision-making is largely intuitive rather than analytical. Things are decided more by hunch or by feel than through lengthy analysis. Hiring is based on a feeling that this person will fit in and this person won't.

- The young school has a family atmosphere about it. Everyone contributes as he or she is able, and most teachers, staff members, and families have a strong sense of loyalty to the school and a sense of camaraderie toward each other. Later, this sense of informal cohesion dissipates, and people speak longingly of the old days, of painting classrooms together, of endless weeks preparing for the fair or of the struggle to find enough money to buy desks.

- The goals and direction of the new school are largely implicit —carried in the minds and hearts of the carrying group of founding teachers and parents. This is not to say that Waldorf education is not talked about, but rather that spelling out in detail the many aspects of what kind of a Waldorf school it will be is rightly seen as unnecessary. It would be a bit like asking a seven-year-old to tell you with precision what he or she will do when grown up.[7]

This childhood phase of a school's life is exciting, somewhat insecure, and very creative. It is a period in which something is developed out of an idea, and then gradually becomes a school with children, teachers, building and playground. One is really bringing a child into the world, a child with a unique personality and full of potential. Very often, one has a feeling of being helped, as if a spiritual being wishes to have an abode on earth and is doing its best to make this possible. I believe this is indeed the case and that developing a school is a process of providing a body or a sheath for a spiritual being to enter into earth evolution. Consequently, the motive and aims of the school founders and their proper grounding in Waldorf pedagogy are important in determining what types of spiritual beings are called to it. Seen from this perspective, the childhood, or pioneer phase of a school, is the time when the first home, or physical body of the school, is created.

Childhood Illnesses

In the same way that children have childhood diseases, new schools face challenges and difficulties analogous to bouts of illness. They are seldom fatal, and they can serve to strengthen the school if worked with. A few of the more common childhood illnesses of new Waldorf schools are:

- The pioneer or godparent who wants a Waldorf school helps it to get started and partially funds the initiative, but is not existentially involved. The help often comes with strings attached, and the person may seek to control the hiring and development of the school. While the motives are usually positive, unless the person actually works in the school and gradually gives up his or her authority to a faculty group and Board, endless difficulties ensue.

- The golden spoon is a similar difficulty. If one or two people fund an initiative, automatically covering its deficits, then the school never has to articulate its purpose and generate support from a wider parent and community group. This situation is analogous to being excessively pampered—it spoils one and leads to not facing reality.

- The over-planned and "perfect Waldorf school" has everything so planned out that the reality of the local setting and its needs are never seen or heard. Such an orientation creates a school incapable of responding to needs and opportunities, a school too rigid and ideological to have a living dialogue with children, parents, and environment.

- The reverse of the "perfect Waldorf school" is a new school whose commitment to Waldorf education is so loose that it becomes an alternative school, attempting to cater to the wishes of a very diverse parent community. Sooner or later this creates an atmosphere where no one is happy since each group has a different picture of what the school should be.

- The perfect home syndrome occurs when a young school group finds the ideal site, suitable for the next seven years, but it is expensive. The group then spends all its human and financial energy on the site before the school is actually established.

- The balanced sharing of responsibility in the life of a school is one of the most common areas of conflict as a school grows. If the school was started by a strong parent group, there is the need to give a growing teacher body responsibility for all areas of the pedagogy, including hiring. If it was started by teachers, the challenge is one of creating a Board and parent association which have real involvement in areas of finance, publicity, outreach, and a host of other areas necessary to support the education. In either case, it is a question of learning to openly share responsibility for the well being of the initiative.

As these and other developmental difficulties are overcome, the school will grow in strength and size. Above all, it will begin to feel as if it is here to stay. The early dramas of enrollment, teacher recruitment and financial deficits still appear, but one doesn't have the feeling that they are life threatening. Indeed after five, six, seven or more years, a sense of continuity, growth and confidence exists.

A Time of Transition

A period of "relative" tranquillity of an understood order and way of doing things may go on for quite a number of years. Yet as the initiative grows, with six, seven or eight grades, a new group of questions and concerns appear. Partly this is connected to size; with over 100 children and many full- and part-time teachers, the old feeling of intimacy disappears. New teachers and parents join the school who have not shared the joys and struggles of the early days and who have no relation to the school's past or to many of the people who made the school what it is. Indeed, they begin to resent the myths and sagas of the heroic old days.

In many schools this transition phase from childhood to adulthood manifests itself through a typical set of issues. One of these is a loss of confidence in existing leadership. Criticism is heard, usually from newer teachers or parents, about the "autocratic," "arbitrary" or "irrational" manner in which decisions are made. Such criticism also points to unclarity about goals, policies and direction. Earlier in the history of the school there was a direct, personal relationship between members of the school community. Most people knew whom to go to when an issue arose. As this breaks down, a need for clearly articulated goals and policies is perceived, and in their absence, questions likely to arise are: "What are the disciplinary procedures in the school? How is teacher evaluation and hiring carried out? What role do Board and teachers play in the establishment of the budget?"

A connected question that arises in this transitional time is the nature of teacher-parent relationships. If the faculty of a Waldorf school carries full educational responsibility for the curriculum, for teaching activities and for teacher hiring and evaluation, what is the role of the parent in the life of a school? How does a parent move from being interested in the school and supporting Waldorf education to being a member of the Finance Committee or the Board of Trustees?

Another frequently expressed concern is the inadequacy of administrative practices. In the early years, parents, teachers, spouses or friends helped in the office, answered phones and carried out a large variety of administrative work. Now the workload, the need for more adequate records, and for financial expertise require more help. The call for professionalism of office and administration is indeed a need that requires at least one full-time person, preferably someone with both a deep understanding of Waldorf education and experience in financial and administrative matters.

These issues, and others, in combination, produce a crisis of confidence that is both perplexing and painful for the school community. As in adolescence, the need for change and development is recognized, but its direction appears obscure. It is in such circumstances that developmental pictures can help, not as a prescription, but as a perspective which outlines the contours of the next possible landscape.

Adulthood: Differentiation with Clarity

The challenge in this phase of a school's development is how to achieve greater clarity and a better division of responsibility so that a larger, more complex organization can thrive. In the early years, getting started and surviving were paramount. Now, the task is permeating the school's life with a new consciousness that allows more functional differentiation without sacrificing individual creativity and commitment. I believe that achieving this balance and entering a healthy differentiation process involves paying attention to a number of inter-connected elements, some of which have been touched on. One important need for the school at this stage of its evolution is renewing its identity and purpose by developing a shared vision of the future and a clear mission statement. This means a renewed dialogue with the original intention, with the spirit of the school. What was our original vision and what is it now? Do we wish to develop a full Waldorf school, K-12, or just K-8? It is not enough to say we want a Waldorf school now, but what kind of a Waldorf school, with what qualities, and in what setting? To involve faculty, Board, parents and friends in a longer discussion of the future can focus the will and generate enthusiasm toward the work needing to be done.[8]

In addition to a picture of the future and a mission statement, the faculty and Board of the school need to become clearer about policies so that a division and delegation of responsibilities can occur. As schools move into this phase of development, committees proliferate; and yet, frequently they are not allowed to really work, since the faculty or the College of Teachers wants to be involved in every decision. This is not the

31

result of perversity, but rather that committees do not have access to clearly articulated policies on the host of issues affecting the life of the school. Policies are statements of value preference, and they should have the full support of the faculty and, in many cases, the Board. For example, what is the basis for teacher salaries? Is an experienced teacher with Waldorf training a priority? Is a part of the policy on teacher hiring to inquire about the relation to Anthroposophy? What is the policy on scholarships, on expulsion, on drug abuse? Is there a clear policy on teacher evaluation and development? Each of these areas requires value judgments. If these judgments have not been discussed, agreed to and embodied in policies, a committee has no basis for action. To my mind, the absence of clear policies undermines the vitality and life of many Waldorf schools, because it means that committees cannot work and that both faculty and College meetings are clogged up with a multitude of detailed issues that limit pedagogical and spiritual work.

As mentioned, an important principle in this phase of school development is that of giving clear tasks to committees and individuals.[9] If policies have been established, then the function, tenure and reporting responsibilities of committees can be defined and a form of *republican leadership* exercised.[10] The following types of committees are common in most established schools:

Faculty	Board
Pedagogical Committee Enrollment Hiring and Teacher Evaluation Festivals and Special Events Administrative Committee	Finance and Budget Tuition Assistance Long-Term Planning Development

Republican leadership, however, requires trust, or at least the discipline of letting others do a task differently than you would have done it. To do so runs counter to the democratic urge to be involved in everything. It may be good to remind ourselves that the Founding Fathers in the United States, in their wisdom, framed a constitution based on republican principles of delegated powers and responsibilities. I have sometimes attended faculty meetings and looked at the agenda to see a host of issues listed which should have been worked through by committee—such as vacation schedules and playground safety.

Another aspect of the need for functional specialization and clarifying structural relationships is the necessity of defining the roles and relationships of the main decision-making bodies in the life of the school. This includes the College of Teachers or Faculty Council, the administrative council, the Faculty Meeting, the Board of Trustees, and the Parent-Teacher Association. Clarifying parent-teacher relationships is an important part of this task. In many Waldorf schools the quality of teacher-parent relations has not received sufficient attention, which leads to many misunderstandings and conflicts.[11] To talk about "teacher run schools" without being clear about the ways in which all the members of the school community are responsible and accountable to each other is not adequate and has been the source of many unnecessary misunderstandings in Waldorf schools.

An additional dimension of the differentiation phase in the life of a school is the need for a change in leadership and decision-making styles. In most new schools leadership is personal and decisions are made by hunch, based on a kind of intuition. As the school grows, leadership needs to become more functionally related to areas of expertise and responsibility. People need to be asked to take on different leadership responsibilities based on competence, not on who is willing. A volunteer principle is appropriate in the early years of a school's life, but no longer when it is well-established. The Board chair, the school's Treasurer, the Faculty and College Chairs should, for example, all be selected based on an understanding of the job and on an awareness of the personal qualities and job skills of potential nominees. The best way to choose people based on competence is to elaborate criteria for the position together on the Faculty or Board and to then ask a nominating committee to recommend a candidate. A common mistake which schools make is to choose a chairperson who is quite outspoken, a "leader" but someone who in fact does not have a strong process or facilitating capacity.

At the same time, decision-making needs greater rationality and consciousness. Both leadership and decision-making will develop over time, but the transition is often difficult as individuals used to the freer, less defined approach of the early years resent the more rational and sometimes more "bureaucratic" approach of the differentiation phase.

If the above-mentioned needs of renewed vision, clearer policies, differentiated structures and committee systems, and a transformed style of leadership and decision-making are met, then the school can enter a healthy differentiation process in which new forms are balanced by a new, more "administrative" consciousness. Yet many Waldorf schools consciously resist meeting these administrative questions, either because of limited organizational experience or because teachers do not have the time, energy, or inclination to come to grips with these types of questions. In the same way that early adulthood calls on a different awareness than adolescence, so, too, will the complexity of a growing school require a greater organizational awareness.

When the school enters the differentiation phase, as many Waldorf schools have, it manifests some or all of the following qualities:

1. Increased size and complexity
2. Clearer policies and procedures
3. Differentiated structures, with a clear committee system
4. A higher level of expertise and more specialization and professionalism in administrative areas
5. More functional leadership, with greater dispersal of responsibilities
6. More rational modes of decision-making
7. Greater clarity of work activities

One can view a school as a living being requiring the maintenance of three dialogues for its health. The first dialogue is with the spirit, with the ideals of Waldorf education and with the spiritual being of the school. The second necessary dialogue is with the human and social environment, with parents, children, friends, and with the community. The third dialogue is with the earth, with finances, administration, buildings and grounds. The administrative focus of the differentiation phases emphasizes the dialogue with the earth, and this emphasis must be consciously balanced by paying attention to spiritual ideals and to human relationships.[12]

The phase of differentiation may go on for many years in a school's life. Its emphasis on clarity and rationality suggests that this period is analogous to early and middle adulthood.

The long-term limitations of an administrative phase, when attention and consciousness are rightly focused inward, are very visible to those individuals working in large corporations or governmental bureaucracies. But they also manifest in older Waldorf schools, in hospitals and in other smaller but well-established institutions. The weight of the past and of tradition, the number of endless meetings, a lack of purpose and leadership, the absence of innovation and a growing sense of mediocrity are the most common concerns. Being well-established and in most cases quite secure, it is as if the school were experiencing a kind of mid-life crisis, in which the search for new meaning and a new way of working become critical. Often part of the crisis of the administrative phase in Waldorf schools is that the same group of teachers has been together so long that they are no longer creative with each other or that the more innovative teachers have left leaving those with less initiative.

Maturity: A Conscious Community of Learning, Meeting and Service

Bernard Lievegoed refers to the third major phase of a school's or a spiritual organization's life as a time of flowering.[13] To bring about such a flowering, I believe, requires meeting three major challenges if the school is to avoid the dangers of mediocrity and decline. These challenges are now not so much external as internal. Usually the school will own its buildings, have a reasonable enrollment and a certain level of financial stability. It will also have developed traditions and habits, which are both assets and liabilities.

The first challenge is that of becoming a conscious learning community. A teaching culture runs the risk of being devoted to knowledge acquired in the past and to imparting that knowledge to others. While this is indeed essential, over time we can become comfortable and not open to new inquiry. We may even resent other Waldorf schools' efforts to work with the grade school curriculum or with adolescence differently than we do. The first part of becoming a conscious learning community involves deepening the spiritual, meditative and pedagogical work of teachers. Can we bring to consciousness, and can we share and renew our commitment to the path of individual inner development and to the principles of Waldorf education? Can faculty or College meetings create time for individual teachers to explore with others what is working for them and what is not? Strengthening and enlivening the joint meditations of teachers in the College meeting is very important.

A part of becoming a conscious learning community is to inaugurate a conscious professional development plan for all teachers and staff. Can the school every year ask each teacher and full-time staff person to develop a personal and professional development plan in which the goals of inner and outer development are articulated and shared? Such goals could be briefly shared in the faculty-staff meeting or the College meeting and worked on in more detail with the personnel committee. Questions to consider are: What are the personal qualities I want to develop this year (perhaps more patience and inner discipline);

what are the social qualities (better listening and facilitation skills); and what are the professional teaching skills (better blackboard drawings, more facility at singing or a better sense of discipline)? The visits of master teachers and the attendance at professional conferences and workshops would then have a conscious and integrated learning and development focus.

Another aspect of becoming a conscious learning community is to develop a conscious learning and review process for all organs of the school's life. As all development activities require extra effort and consciousness, perhaps a Learning Mandate group could be established to coordinate and stimulate activity. Do the mandate groups have a conscious learning and review process? A good pattern is to review or evaluate every meeting briefly. Have we achieved our aims? What was the mood of our gathering, how was speaking and listening? This need not be more than five minutes, although in form it needs to be consciously varied in order to avoid boredom and routine. Every semester a longer review of functioning can be established. How is the Finance Committee working? What are the strengths and weaknesses of the Faculty and Staff meeting? What can we do to improve things? This applies to the Board, the Parent Association and the faculty and staff. Then every year, perhaps after the close of school, a Learning Forum could be held to assess the achievements and limitations of the year. Parents, Board, friends, faculty and staff could participate in a kind of learning festival in which different aspects of the school's life can be explored for learning and improvement. In any type of learning effort, the mood is not one of blaming, but of saying what we can learn from these successes and these failures. This type of annual retreat can generate hope, for it allows the naming of issues but with the purpose of improvement, learning, and growth.

A Culture of Partnership

The second major challenge of becoming a mature school community is to develop a true culture of partnership and of meeting. A school is a destiny community of children, teachers, parents, staff and supporters. How can this recognition find form and substance? The first requirement is that we consciously recognize this destiny partnership and honor it. At the heart of this question is the relationship between teachers and children, staff, and parents. The teachers give their knowledge, care, and love of the education and of the child, the administration supports the education and makes it possible practically, the parents entrust their

36

child and in the case of Waldorf schools, provide the financial resources to support the education. This relationship finds expression in the organs of the school's life, in the College of Teachers, in the faculty/staff meeting, in the Parent Association, in the Board and in class evenings. Can the partnership be made fully conscious in agreements on rights and responsibilities? Each family as part of its annual contract could agree to a statement of rights and responsibilities which goes beyond financial matters and discipline, and also describes expected levels of involvement in the class, in parent evenings, of membership in the School Association and participation in festivals, committees, and Board. It would describe the rights and responsibilities of teachers in making all personnel and pedagogical decisions, of the Board in making financial and legal decisions and of the School Association in having the task of providing a dialogue forum for issues such as school schedules, tuition levels and financial assistance, in major development and capital projects, and perhaps in areas such as disciplinary procedures and mediation of difficulties. Equally, the teachers would sign an annual agreement that would describe rights and responsibilities. An important part of such an agreement is describing not only the pedagogical responsibilities but agreeing to attend certain meetings, agreeing to committee assignments and an annual assessment or review process as part of ongoing professional development and evaluation. Not long ago I experienced a situation in which a faculty member refused to attend faculty meetings saying they were too stressful and also refused to work through her difficulties with colleagues. Without a written contract to rely on, her colleagues were criticized as being "arbitrary" and "punitive" when they tried to insist on her participation. Freedom to teach in the classroom needs to be consciously balanced by agreements on rights and responsibilities as professional colleagues. This includes being clear about codes of conduct between colleagues and between teachers and children.[14]

Agreements on rights and responsibilities between teachers/staff and parents can be supplemented by agreements with children in the High School, in areas of dress code, substance abuse, disciplinary procedures, and the responsibility for monitoring such agreements can be given to a mixed faculty-student group.

The inner side of the challenge of partnership is the question of how to foster true meetings between human beings. This is increasingly difficult in a time when our general culture promotes egotism and social fragmentation. As Rudolf Steiner notes repeatedly, we are increasingly isolated from each other as individuals, yet we long for community.[15] His answer to the question of a deeper meeting is that we need new social forms which help us to become conscious of our interdependence, and we need to develop a new practical social understanding which creates interest between people.[16] Waldorf school communities are new social forms, but they require a high level of social understanding and skill to work effectively. I sometimes think we have been given the legacy of new social forms, but bring little consciousness to the art of social creation, while conventional organizations have old forms, but struggle mightily with a new social consciousness and skill to make them work. Servant leadership, group facilitation and communication skills, decision-making by consensus, mediation processes, teamwork, and a service orientation are attitudes and skills that the more conventional world is busily acquiring. We have much to learn in this regard, so that we can develop a social art that facilitates the building of healthy communities. I believe a systematic learning in communication skills, in group facilitation, in conflict resolution, and in biography work as well as in the arts of promoting healthy family life is essential if Waldorf schools are to fulfill their promise of becoming seeds for a new society. The methods and approaches for acquiring such new social skills are readily available, but we need to overcome our prejudices and be willing to learn.

Mature schools can consciously pick up this challenge and, in so doing, develop a spiritually inspired social art that can facilitate the experience of community. Consciously sharing aspects of an individual's biography, having both a chairperson and a process coach who intervenes only in times of difficulty and helps in group review, practicing listening exercises and paraphrasing, having moments where teachers share that which they are working and struggling with in the classroom, beginning and ending in a moment of silence, are all methods with which we can work consciously. They will help to bring about more life and a deeper meeting between individuals.

Underlying the question of meeting skills is the question of how we deal with our difficulties and disagreements. Learning to name them, taking responsibility for our difficulty with each other, all of us acquiring mediation and feedback skills, are essential so that the unspoken judgments and untruths don't block our meeting. Individually we can picture our colleagues, note their strengths and weaknesses, and remember when we have experienced something of their striving individuality. This activity and intention is beautifully expressed in Rudolf Steiner's reflections on Faithfulness:

Create for yourself a new, indomitable perception of faithfulness. What is usually called faithfulness passes so quickly. Let this be your faithfulness:

You will experience moments - fleeting moments - with the other person. The human being will appear to you then as if filled, irradiated with a spirit archetype.

And then there may be - indeed, will be - other moments, long periods of time when human beings are darkened. But you will learn to say to yourself at such times: "The Spirit makes me strong. I remember the archetype. I saw it once. No illusion, no deception shall rob me of it."

Always struggle for the image that you saw. This struggle is faithfulness. Striving thus for faithfulness, we shall be close to one another, as if endowed with the protective power of angels.

- Rudolf Steiner

A Service Culture

The school is also a part of a wider community, its local region, and the community of Waldorf schools. What responsibility and what opportunity for service does the school have in its local community? Does it, should it, make its festivals available to local groups? Can it open its festivals to other communities? Is there the opportunity for civic engagement, for adult education, for local volunteer and service activities? It is good if a teacher is a member of the local Rotary club, or of the volunteer Ambulance Corp. Is the school a member of the National Association of Independent Schools, and of the Association of Waldorf Schools of North America (AWSNA)? The mature Waldorf school can also reach out and mentor or provide assistance to new fledgling Waldorf schools in the region, or support a public Waldorf inspired initiative. All of these activities of service give life and are part of the potential for flowering. For without this sharing and giving, an inner lassitude can set in so that we fail to recognize the many blessings that we have been given. Without service, a culture of mutual criticism, of gossip and of cynicism can develop, which becomes the antithesis of healthy community life.

Part of developing a culture of service is finding new ways of organizing the work of the school community. The second phase of school development is characterized by the differentiation and the gradual professionalization of administration and decision-making forms. The dangers of this phase over time are a gradual fragmentation and loss of direction, characterized by long meetings, many committees and poor coordination and communication. What was carried by the whole faculty and by many committees can now be simplified, streamlined and delegated to a few responsibility or mandate groups. If attention has been paid to a qualitative renewal of the vision and mission of the school and to re-enlivening the pedagogical principles of Waldorf education and to a new understanding of mutual partnership, then the school can look to principles of federation, of creating a smaller number of responsibility groups with substantial autonomy and responsibility. The Toronto Waldorf School and the Pine Hill Waldorf School (NH) have worked on this mode of organizing the work life of their schools for some time. In the case of Toronto, the full faculty is the mandating group to whom the mandate groups report both their issues and their decisions. In the case of Pine Hill, it is the College of Teachers that remains the main policy-making body or in financial matters, the Board of Trustees. Whereas the school before may have had up to ten teacher committees and four or five Board committees, now the school may have just four or five faculty mandate groups that are empowered to make decisions on behalf of the whole, and one or two Board mandate groups. A typical mandate structure for a Waldorf school can have the following kind of form:

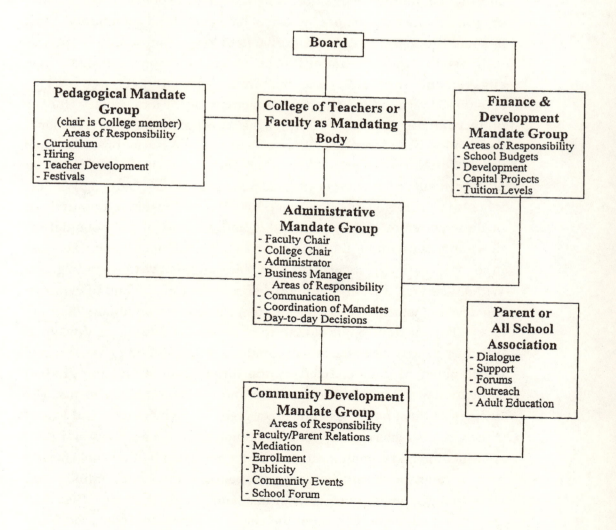

In creating a mandate organization it is imperative to have a mandating body, which can be the full faculty or the College of Teachers or the Board. The mandate areas need to be clearly defined and then the best three to five people chosen to fulfill the tasks. Here the questions should be what combination of people can best be responsible for this area of work on behalf of the whole. They need to have the trust of the faculty and or Board and also be clear about their length of tenure and the policies that govern their area of work. The Pedagogical mandate or responsibility group can only interview potential candidates for teaching positions if it knows what qualities are being looked for in teachers, the level of experience and training, and the spiritual orientation. These are policy and value questions which the faculty or College of Teachers needs to have decided beforehand. Another required area of clarity is what decisions the responsibility group can or cannot make for the whole.

A critical aspect of a mandate organization is the facilitation and coordination of work. This can best be done by a coordinating mandate group that could consist of the Faculty chairperson, the College chairperson, and key administrative staff, perhaps the Business Manager, the Administrator and/or the Development person. The particular forms of a federated, mandate structure will vary from school to school, but the principle of the delegation of decision-making to smaller groups based on the principles of competence and effectiveness is critical, so that the College of Teachers, the Board and the faculty meeting are freed to do their pedagogical or policy setting.

Another task connected to school forms at their mature phase of development is the task of penetrating the social and organizational structure of the school with the insights and ideals of spiritual science. Most Waldorf schools already work with some of these ideals, for example, in their collegial structures of decision-making. Other steps would involve more intensive work with the fundamental social law of Rudolf Steiner in finding a new relation both to salaries and tuition income, or in conscious decision making by consensus. Many schools are moving away from needs-based salaries, because it is too demanding, while others seek conventional solutions to financial and social issues. A deepening study of the social content of Anthroposophy by the faculty and Board, and a more intensive sharing of the innovative practices of other Waldorf schools can become the inspiration for working with threefold principles in new ways.

I believe it is only in true maturity and usually after the middle forties that individuals can give unselfishly to others. Similarly, it is in the phase of maturity, with a new commitment to their spiritual, pedagogical and social ideals that Waldorf schools can become places where individuals and families can find the human, educational and spiritual nourishment so needed in our time.

A Conscious Ending

If the pioneer stage can be likened to childhood, the differentiation phase to early and middle adulthood, and the integration phase to full maturity, what can be said about the death of an initiative? A convenient response is to say that schools die when they fail and are no longer needed. However, I feel that many institutions have not only become old, but also sclerotic, disposing of substantial resources, but no longer really serving human needs. If one pursues the human metaphor, perhaps institutions should only live for three generations or ninety years, if they are to effectively serve the needs of the time. What would happen to cultural, social and economic creativity if institutions over ninety years old, such as Harvard, General Motors or the Catholic Church, turned over their resources to new groups wishing to respond to similar needs in new ways? What a peaceful, on-going, creative revolution society would experience! To do this would require all institutions, including Waldorf schools, to contemplate a conscious death process in order to allow a new resurrection. It is an intriguing thought, if not a present reality, with resistances similar in nature to our individual fear of dying.

The Image of Development

What has been presented is a sketch of developmental patterns in a school's life. Frequently I am asked, "Can't a stage be missed?" The answer is no. Organizations have a life cycle moving from simple to more complex, from one central organizing principle to another. This means that true development is a discontinuous, irreversible process in time, moving from a stage of growth through differentiation to a higher stage of integration and passing through states of crisis which offer the impetus for development. This pattern is, I believe, true for all life forms, for the human being, and for schools and other organizations.

However, it is possible for initiatives to move more or less rapidly through these phases. A school which starts with six grades and a kindergarten will face questions of differentiation much sooner than one which starts with one grade, adding a new grade each year. Furthermore, it is quite common for organizations to have different segments of the institution in different stages of development. A kindergarten and grade

42

school may have entered the differentiation phase, while the school's new high school will be in its childhood pioneering period, and the two parts of the school will feel and function differently. This definitely needs to be appreciated by the many Waldorf schools now developing high schools after 20 or 25 years of existence.

In presenting this picture of school development, a number of complementary images have been alluded to. They can be summarized in the following manner:

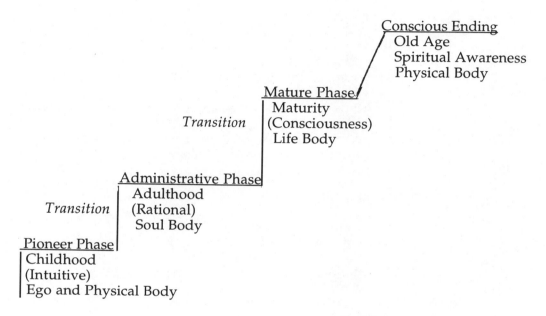

The image of birth, childhood, adulthood, and maturity is a metaphor that is quite clear. The qualities of intuitive, rational and conscious refer to the characteristic ways of approaching the world and of making decisions in the different phases in the life of the initiative.[17] Another way of seeing this development process is to realize that the dialogue with the spirit (identity), the dialogue with people (relationships), and the dialogue with the earth (resources) need to become ever more conscious in the school's life, if the forces of decay and disintegration are not to become dominant over the course of time.

This description of Waldorf school development is both general and incomplete. Like all ideal-type descriptions it cannot do justice to the rich texture of life in the Austin, Minneapolis, Chapel Hill or Lexington Waldorf Schools. Its purpose is rather to describe a landscape of possibilities, indicating paths to be pursued and pitfalls to be avoided so that we may become more conscious co-creators of our school communities.

A Checklist of Questions and Issues for New Waldorf Schools

1. **Recognizing the Vision**

    What is our imagination, our vision for this school?
    Do we have a common image?
    What ideas do we hope to realize?
    How do we relate to Waldorf education and to Anthroposophy?
    What changes will the school bring about in our lives, in our
        children's lives, and in the community?

2. **Answering a Need**

    Is there a need for a Waldorf school in our community, and how
        do we know this?
    Are there sufficient numbers of children and parents interested in
        Waldorf education?
    What needs and wishes does the community express about
        education?
    What do these expressions of interest say about the opportunities
        and limitations we face in starting a Waldorf school?

3. **Formulating a Direction**

    What will be the name of the school?
    What image of the school do we wish to promote and realize over
        the next two to three years?
    What activities will we foster over the next few years to nurture
        and support the school?
    What kind of brochure should we have?

4. **Commitment of People**

    Who is committed to the initiative and why?
    Who is in the initiative group and who can be counted on for the
        long haul?
    Who are the supporters?
    Is the general community aware and supportive of the school?
    Is there financial support?

5. **Organizing our Work Together**

    What are the right legal forms for us?
    How are we going to organize the school, the association, the
        Board, faculty, and parent group?
    Who will make what decisions and how will decisions be
        communicated between various groups?
    How will we relate to supporters, Board members, parent
        community and town?
    What financial arrangements will we make for tuition income and
        for salaries?

6. Work Activities

What are the central work activities needed in the school:
teaching, office, public relations, fund-raising, etc.?
What are our priorities?
Who will do what?
How will work be coordinated and by whom?
What do we see as volunteer work and what as paid work?

7. Finding Facilities and Resources

What building space and equipment will we need now and in
three-to-five years?
What quality of environment do we wish to create for children
and teachers?
Do we have a capital budget?
Do we have the intention of building a new school or buying an
existing one?
How are we going to deal with the usual operating deficit?
Is there a fund-raising and development committee?
Do we have a development plan for the future?[6]

This essay first appeared in *Economic Explorations*. 1988, pp. 19-35, and has been updated and modified.

[1] Rudolf Steiner, GA, 93, p. 130, translated by the author from the German.

[2] This essay is adapted from C. Schaefer and T. Voors, *Vision in Action: Working with the Soul and Spirit in Small Organizations*. Lindisfarne Press, 2nd Edition, 1996.

[3] Both the picture of school development given and the various examples cited are based on many years of work by the author with Waldorf schools in the United States, Canada, and the United Kingdom.

[4] See L.E. Grenier, *Evolution and Revolution as Organizations Grow*, Harvard Business Review, July-August, 1972.

[5] A.C. Harwood, *The Recovery of Man in Childhood*. Anthroposophic Press, 1982.

[6] This question list is adapted and modified from *Vision in Action*.

[7] See Bernard Lievegoed, *The Developing Organization*, pp. 55-61, Tavistock Publications, 1973. Published by Celestial Arts, 1979. Also, *Developing Communities*. Hawthorne Press, 1995.

[8] See Christopher Schaefer, *Developing an Image of the Future: A Long-Term Planning Process for Waldorf Schools*, available from Sunbridge College.

[9] See *Vision in Action*, pp. 81-88, on giving mandates to committees.

[10] See the excellent essay by Ernst Lehrs, *Republican Not Democratic*, available from the Association of Waldorf Schools of North America.

[11] See Manfred Leist, *Parent Participation in the Life of a Waldorf School*, available from the Association of Waldorf Schools of North America.

[12] The concept of these dialogues and of the threefold picture of the school is elaborated in *Vision in Action*, pp. 61-63.

[13] Bernard Lievegoed, *Developing Communities*. Hawthorne Press, 1995.

[14] See the excellent articles by Heinz Zimmermann, "What Conditions Are there for Taking Responsibility in an Independent Life of Culture," *What Is Happening in the Anthroposophical Society*, 17.4 and 18.1, 1996, 1997.

[15] Rudolf Steiner, *Social and Anti-Social Forces in the Human Being*. Mercury Press.

[16] Rudolf Steiner, *How Can the Soul Needs of the Time Be Met?*. Zurich, October 10, 1946.

Chapter 4

Financial and Strategic Planning for Waldorf Schools

by

Ann Stahl

There are three elements to consider in planning for the healthy financial development of a Waldorf school: the financial, the strategic, and the pedagogical. Financial planning cannot happen without a strategic plan, and neither can function in a vacuum. Both must be informed and led by the pedagogical vision re-enlivened each year in the life of the school.

Planning is crucial to the healthy growth of any endeavor, and the activity includes the individuals, both paid and volunteer, who are part of that organism. Over time, planning extends beyond the immediate organism to the wider community and the world. Financial planning is one aspect of the various kinds of planning needed for the health of the organization. Strategic, or long range planning, is another.

A plan is the form that describes an alive and lively process, capturing it for a day or week or month or year, sometimes for three to five years. The process of arriving at a plan reflects the ever-changing life of the organism, whether it is a single human being, a large corporation or a cultural endeavor such as the Waldorf school. Planning recognizes and considers new challenges, new possibilities and new thinking as these come to awareness in individuals and in various parts of the organization over time.

Planning of all kinds, including financial and strategic, is the responsibility of those people who step forward or who are recognized and asked to assume that responsibility for a period of time in the life of the organization. Initiative taking, or leadership, can arise from the center of the organization (in the case of Waldorf schools from the faculty or

College of Teachers) or from the periphery (parents taking an active volunteer role on the Board or its committees).

The skills and vision needed for financial planning are most often found within the volunteer parent body of the school. The vision for the long-range pedagogical (or strategic) plan emanates from the faculty or College of Teachers. These two aspects of the school, working together as a hand in a glove (or perhaps as bat and ball!), inform each other and help move the school forward towards its stated goals.

Visioning

The main characteristic of a healthy organism, be it a single human being, a corporation or a Waldorf school, is a deeply understood and clearly articulated task. Why am I here? Why are we here? What is our purpose and work together? Recognizing and formulating the impulse that brought the school into being will serve, ever and again, as the guiding star which can be seen and recognized by the ever-growing community that surrounds the school and begins to shine out into the wider community and the world.

Organizations with unclear motives resemble chariots without drivers—moving, but haphazardly, and in danger of losing a wheel. The school's stated vision and goals that follow from them serve as foundation, as well as guiding star, for all planning. The future can be served from the vantage point of standing in the present moment, insofar as the organization is able to reflect upon and understand its past. If all three vistas are achieved, vibrancy and visibility will be evident. This points to the never-ending activity of review and reflection, hopefully on a yearly basis, by the College of Teachers, faculty and Board and shared with the larger community. Without this vital spiritual/practical work, the organism cannot maintain clear direction in planning for its healthy unfolding.

Strategic Planning

The strategic plan reflects the vision and goals, both short-term and long-range, articulated by the leadership of the faculty/College and the Board. The vision informs the goals which are further articulated into discernible parts, into recognizable "bundles of work," which may include site selection, building plans, renovation plans, finding of faculty and staff, fund raising, coordinating volunteers, and so forth.

Do the founders want a city school, or is a school with a farm envisioned? Is it to be a one-room all-grades rural school or a full kindergarten through grade twelve able to serve children with mild to moderate learning difficulties? What about a four-day school with parents taking responsibility for the learning on the fifth day?

It is easy to see that each of the above models will require a unique plan of realization, from the spaces that will be purchased or rented to the number and variety of teachers needed. Is there a choice of sites available? Where is the right location? What is the plan for site selection? Is affordability a factor? What is the time line for securing the site? How and by whom will the decision on site be made? How many teachers will be hired? How many children will need to be enrolled to support the hiring of a teacher, or additional teachers?

If the plan is for one year only, how is the second year of existence seen? Is the intention to carry the initiative into the future? How many kindergarten children can be served in one class? Where will we find the next teacher? Shall we rent or buy a space that has potential to serve growth for one year, two, five? Where do we want to be in three years? All of these questions can be "bundled" into task components and mandated by the Board for further work by smaller groups.

A key vision statement component with strong financial implications is the one concerning the school's intention to include or to try to include all those families who want to have a Waldorf education for their children. Much unhappiness and strife have resulted from misunderstanding or miscommunicating this vision into the strategic and financial plans of the school. Another key component of the strategic plan is whether or not the faculty will request the financial support required to live in the area in which the school is located.

Questions such as these point to the necessity of active work and deliberation by the faculty/College and the Board together. The faculty/College can come to major decisions dictated by the vision in isolation. The response of the Board can then become adversarial since its task is primarily oriented towards the financial health of the school. The separate components of the strategic plan relate to the organism as a whole. The ability to balance perceived needs with existing resources is part of the creative tension and possibility (and the fun) of daily life in the strong yet delicate organism known as a Waldorf school.

All these questions and many others will guide the strategic planning of the organization. It is easy to see that for each aspect of the strategic plan a corresponding financial reality must be in place to support it.

Financial Planning

The first act of any new organization which continues throughout its lifetime is to construct a yearly plan which includes a balanced operating budget. Achieving the balance between the goals of the strategic plan and the realities of the financial plan is the responsibility of the Board of Trustees with the help of its finance committee. This important committee, usually comprised of parent volunteers with the necessary skills and expertise, is sometimes joined by a faculty/College member as well. With the support of the strategic plan as its mandate along with achieving a balance between the inflow of revenue and the outflow of expenses, it is clear that the work of the finance committee in financial planning is not easy!

Each year there are many unknowns and sometimes big surprises. The largest number in the operating budget of any organization is the support needed for personnel. The circulation of money in a Waldorf school flows between the parents and the teachers: parents support the needs of the teachers who take responsibility for the education of the children in their care.

In a school growing by one class each year, the operating budget is relatively simple to construct. It has two main factors, tuition and teacher support (or salaries). If all the children enrolled in the current year return in the next year, enrollment can be predicted by adding the 12-30 new first grade children and estimating the additional revenue, taking into account the amount for tuition assistance and tuition for faculty children. Corresponding expenses include the needs of the new first grade teacher.

The planning picture becomes more complex when enrollment figures are unclear, known to be much lower for the coming year, or in such flux that a reasonable estimate cannot be established. In this case, many finance committees use a "good," "better," "best," scenario with a balanced budget the objective in each case. Many "pieces of the puzzle" may not be readily forthcoming. Not knowing who the new teacher will be may impact the enrollment of that class if families enroll elsewhere due to uncertainty; loss of a teacher almost always affects the balance. Failure to secure a next site before the end of the school year can also seriously impact enrollment and upset the delicate balance of operations.

These circumstances point to the need for an ongoing focus by one person in the area of enrollment as well as to the necessity for the faculty/College to be actively responsible for what is happening in each class from the pedagogical/peer evaluation perspective. Great stress is added to the balance between the strategic and financial plan when either or both of these two key areas of responsibility are neglected.

The task of financial planning becomes more possible to maintain when all is in right relationship between parents and teachers. Questions such as health and retirement benefits and sabbaticals can then be addressed from a place of confidence.

The timing for additional or new facilities can be more easily seen and planned for when growth is stable and can be relied upon. A decision to move from a rented to purchased site is a major one and includes planning for a capital campaign to provide the gift money needed. Such a move can be traumatic if the time needed to carry out the financial plan is not sufficient to the task. Good expertise and help is available from within the Waldorf movement and from outside consultants when this event in the life of a school is imminent.

The subject of gift money must not be forgotten in the strategic and financial plan for any initiative in the cultural realm. In addition to the surpluses created by ongoing social events in the life of the school, such as festivals and fairs, the spirit of philanthropy must be cultivated through the school's annual giving campaign. Insofar as the vision and goals of the school are realized and can be seen, gift money will be attracted to ensure the future. Here, too, the dedication and focus of one individual, with the aid of many helpers, will provide the planned-for results.

The three activities of visioning, strategic planning, and financial planning, if practiced rigorously, will provide a healthy financial basis for any initiative. These three, each strong in its own right and pulling in the same direction, will carry the initiative to the realization of its agreed-upon intentions.

Chapter 5

Towards an Economics of Development

by

John Bloom

Development means so much—growth, evolution, maturation as an individual and community process, transforming the latent into the visible, raising money—that it eludes a simple or singular reading. Given the challenges of working in an anthroposophical endeavor such as a Waldorf school, one should study and understand its intention, its necessity, the particular purpose of development, and, especially, the quality of relationships that are at the center of it.

Without grasping development as a metamorphic process, we would not have an understanding of the human being. Without development we would not have a reason to form a picture of the possible. Without development and healthy relations, an organization would fail economically. And, of course, relationships unfold and transform over time. They have a history, live in the present, unfold in the future.

A Waldorf school, for example, has a spiritual and cultural mission: the education of children and their preparation to be citizens of the world. The fulfillment of that mission depends upon a real and sustainable economy. As an activity, development bridges the cultural and the economic realms through the milieu of the school's social life— through the cultivation of relationships and trust. From this perspective it is important to understand the role money plays in and for the school and to reconsider how parents might view their financial relationship to the school.

Often families are asked to participate financially in three ways. First there is tuition, an annual assessment. Second, there are possible loans or bonds, paid before or as one starts paying tuition. Third, there is giving beyond tuition—whether through volunteering, Annual Fund, loan forgiveness, pledges of capital, or deferred gifts through estate planning. The timing and gesture of each of these three modes is different, and each reflects a different facet of financial participation.

Tuition is relatively simple; it has a one year half-life. It is the basis of an independent school's operations, is paid and used in the present—almost monthly—and it recreates daily the possibility for the students and teachers to fulfill their educational tasks together. While paying tuition may seem like a purchase, it should be considered in a different light. One cannot buy experience; rather, tuition makes the experience possible. One can only have an impression of or sense for its value. From this perspective, tuition is associated very much with the feeling life, which connects us to the present.

It may well be that a portion of tuition goes toward servicing debt incurred to purchase land or make building improvements. Whether this is the case, or a school has a revolving loan or bond program, the point is that all of this loan money continues to implement a transaction that happened in the past. It more or less consciously links each family with the financial aspect of the school's history. The quality of a loan is that in its whole it is entirely conceptual, a formulaic contractual structure based upon projection over time. In its particular it is invariably in a state of change—witness the need for an amortization schedule to map principal and interest at a given moment. The nature of loan money with its temporal and spatial abstraction is a metaphoric expression in economic terms of the human capacity of thinking with its quality of reflection, analysis, and conceptualization.

Gift money, given as a free deed beyond anything that is required, points toward the future. It represents a quality of will and the creation of potential. Gift money is most often tied to the ability to imagine the future, often as the basis for a capital campaign. However, even the Annual Fund allows the school to do more than is just necessary to support the teachers and the education—especially teacher development programs that are a real investment in human renewal and growth.

The parallel between the qualities of money and those of the human being engenders a sense for the characteristics of important parts of the school's or organization's economy—loans, tuition, and gifts. Just as we strive in human development for a balance of thinking, feeling, and willing, a healthy organizational economy also requires a balanced distribution of the three kinds of money that it needs and attracts. Too much in the past, or too much in loan and debt, encumbers an organization's development. Too much total dependence on tuition or membership income means being too much in the present, lacking a sense of history and of preparation for the future. Too much focus on gifts and the future tends to jeopardize present operations and devalue the school's history. It may seem odd, but in this schema, debt is a constructive tool provided it is balanced with the other aspects of money. It may also explain why it is nearly impossible to raise money for deficit reduction.

I use the example of Waldorf schools because they stand in the public and primarily serve families unfamiliar with anthroposophical economic thinking. However, money is an educational opportunity in itself, and financial planning an opportune arena for reflection, assessment, and anticipation—for thinking, feeling, and willing together, fully integrated but each with its particular characteristic. I hope this approach to an economics of development offers a tool for looking at the health of an organization from its economy to its human activity—from its outer material expression to its inner, spiritual life.

Chapter 6

On Enrollment

by

Abraham Entin

According to the 1997-98 AWSNA survey, enrollment at Waldorf schools in North America averages 40 students below capacity. As Agaf Dancy (Administrative Coordinator of AWSNA) put it, *"This is without a doubt the most serious challenge facing our schools today, both financially and with respect to the schools' mission to serve the greatest number of students."*

In the past, many of our schools operated on principles of what I would call "anti-enrollment," or "karmic marketing." This is the view that, "if it is a person's destiny to find Waldorf education, he or she will do so." According to this viewpoint, there is something wrong, or "unspiritual," in consciously marketing our schools to the public.

And yet, we know that the adversary forces which oppose Waldorf education do everything they can to blind humanity to the presence of Spirit in the world, and attempt to divert human beings from realizing their true nature and destiny. We also know that, in a Michaelic age, it is up to us as human beings to take responsibility for our own evolution and the destiny of our world.

In view of this, I believe it is both necessary and correct for us to work responsibly and professionally to bring the ideas of Waldorf education to the widest possible public. In doing so, we will also build enrollment and strengthen our schools.

The fact that a separate chapter "On Enrollment" is included in this revised edition of *Economic Explorations* speaks volumes on the new attitude towards enrollment work emerging within the Waldorf schools.

Enrollment and Strategic Planning

Waldorf schools should consider including "Full Enrollment" as an articulated goal and organizing principle of their Strategic Plan for the following reasons:

1. Full enrollment is a reflection that the school is functioning at or close to optimum capability. In order to achieve full enrollment, the school must rely heavily on positive "word of mouth" from current parents and must be successful in meeting the educational needs of its students. In this sense, enrollment can serve as a very accurate reflection of the social and functional health of the institution.

2. Full enrollment will yield the maximum operating income, enabling the school to reach subsidiary but crucial goals, such as maximizing teachers' salaries and benefits, offering the most comprehensive program, and so on.

A certain minimum income is needed to meet the basic personnel and site related expenses of the school. After this point, additional revenue becomes more "discretionary" in nature. When schools operate on lean budgets, due to shortfalls in tuition income, all the programs suffer, and the teachers tend to carry the school through their sacrifice or support. This is debilitating to their personal lives and the programs of the school, and also leads to further shortfalls in the number of qualified teachers and staff to serve the expanding needs of the movement. The healthiest way to reverse this, at individual schools and throughout the school movement, is to operate at or close to full enrollment.

3. Full enrollment demonstrates to the larger community that the school and the education it offers are highly valued. This makes obtaining support and benefits from this larger community substantially more likely.

4. Full enrollment will begin to build the internal base for support, as well as an alumni body, which can support the school and Waldorf education into the future.

Points 3 and 4 point to the fact that enrollment is the basis for healthy development work. The more people who are served by the school, the easier it is to raise other, non-tuition based income to support new buildings, new programs and other efforts on the part of the institutions.

5. Full enrollment maximizes the support which the schools can give to the movement as a whole through the work of the Association of Waldorf Schools. AWSNA dues are currently calculated on a "per student" basis. Healthy enrollment, therefore, means that more resources will be available for programs and efforts which support the movement as a whole, and which make an increasing involvement with the larger community more possible. In this way, the influence of Waldorf education as a force in cultural life is enhanced.

The Enrollment Director

The "de-emphasis" on enrollment efforts is reflected in the fact that relatively few schools have a full time, dedicated enrollment director or coordinator. By dedicated is meant a person whose sole responsibility lies in this area, and who does not carry admissions, development or any other administrative or teaching responsibilities in the school.

While many young schools find themselves in a position where "everyone does everything," the job of meeting new families and maximizing enrollment is a full time job, no matter how young or "undeveloped" a school may be. Indeed, from a certain perspective the younger and less the developed the school, the more necessary it is to make sure that consciousness is focused on this crucial area of school life.

This question of "consciousness" is the crucial component of the job description of the enrollment director. It is the element which informs and provides the underpinning for the specific tasks which are enumerated in the "job description" provided below:

Enrollment Director Job Description
1. To understand the impact of school policies and procedures on the enrollment function, and to communicate that impact in appropriate school forums.

2. To participate in the development of a school marketing plan, and to insure that this plan is implemented and carried out in an effective and efficient manner.

3. To insure that systems are in place to track results of enrollment and outreach events, inquiry calls, interviews, etc., and to track these results.

4. To provide reporting mechanisms which will allow for effective analysis and response based upon these results.

5. To develop enrollment projections, budgets and analyses, and to participate in the school budget development process as directed.

6. To create and maintain databases for mailings and to be familiar with the technological tools which will make the job most effective (or to be the liaison with the person who carries this technological responsibility).

7. To create and participate in activities which directly enhance enrollment and give current parents an opportunity to reaffirm their reasons for choosing Waldorf education.

8. To coordinate staff and volunteers for all enrollment and outreach events.

9. To coordinate publicity, press releases, mailings and so on that directly pertain to outreach and enrollment events.

10. To develop the enrollment event calendar.

11. To develop and build relationships with feeder schools, child care providers and other organizations which can be of assistance in building enrollment.

12. To handle inquiry calls and follow up on all inquiries.

13. To mail appropriate information and follow up.

14. To conduct in person meetings and school tours with prospective families.

15. To arrange teacher/parent interviews and to follow up.

16. To help develop and participate in events and procedures to help new families become an integrated part of the school community.

The above job description is an intensive and extensive list of tasks for a single individual. Items 11, 12 and 14 are the tasks most often associated with the job upon initial reflection. This is where the enrollment director functions as the "public face" of the school, meeting new families and others who are in a position to help build enrollment for the institution. In a certain sense, all the other tasks are in support of these activities.

For these reasons, an ability and desire to represent Waldorf education to the public is the crucial element of the "qualifications" for the position.

The "ability" to represent Waldorf does not, however, mean that one must necessarily be a present or former teacher, or an "expert" on Waldorf pedagogy. Certainly one must be familiar with these aspects, but familiarity as a parent or graduate who has experienced the education personally or through their child, can also serve as a qualification for this position. If an "expert" is necessary for a specific event or meeting, this can be arranged, but an enthusiastic appreciation based upon personal life experience can convey itself to new families in quite a different and effective manner.

The qualities and experiences necessary to carry out all the functions outlined above are many and diverse. In the "ideal" situation, the tasks would be split between an "Enrollment Director" who functioned principally in the "strategic" and "systems" realm, and another individual who concentrated on the "interactive" aspects of the job. Because few (if any) schools are in a position to split the job this way, it is up to the school to find mechanisms of support which recognize the dual nature and extended scope of this position.

Further Institutional Support

Because of the crucial nature of the enrollment function, and because it has been traditionally so "undervalued" by Waldorf schools, it is important that the schools further support enrollment efforts in a variety of crucial ways:

1. The school needs to define "full enrollment" for itself. This will often involve considerations of "optimal class size" as well as physical plant and regulatory considerations. An understanding of the goals involved (how many students are we trying to enroll in a specific class, etc.) is crucial to developing the means of reaching those goals.

In addition, these goals will help the school develop and refine its strategic plan in many other ways. For instance, it may be that increased enrollment is seemingly barred by lack of space for specific subjects (music, eurythmy, etc.) If the school understands the relationship between the revenue(s) provided by increased enrollment and the expenses necessary to serve the additional students, it can make more informed institutional choices about strategies to accommodate this possible growth.

2. The lack of historical support and involvement with enrollment issues on the part of the schools makes faculty education a crucial element in a successful enrollment effort. Current faculty need to understand the pivotal role they play in meeting prospective families and in building enrollment for the school. Similarly, they need to be informed of the benefits accruing to them (in terms of additional support and a stronger program) of a successful enrollment office.

New teachers also need to understand that the school is committed to this process, and that their enthusiastic participation is expected as part of their job. A conversation about this, as well as about the number of students they may be expected to include in their class should be an important element in the interview process. This is stressed because the tendency has been to leave these questions entirely in the hands of the faculty. And yet, if most of the faculty are committed to having "X" number of students in their class, and a few are only willing to accept "X-Y" students, this can cause an unhealthy social situation in the school. The establishment of parameters for class size, along with the recognition that pedagogical concerns will, of course, determine the ultimate configuration of the classroom, are necessary to provide the maximum institutional support for the enrollment function.

3. Finally, a recognition by the Board of Directors of the crucial contribution of enrollment to the financial health of the school should result in a close monitoring of this element of school life, as well as a commitment to oversight and support which will insure the maximum effectiveness of the enrollment office.

Taken together, the above steps can play an important role in creating a healthy enrollment situation, allowing the school to exercise the most freedom in creating a social and pedagogical atmosphere most conducive to the success of the student, the school and the entire Waldorf movement.

Chapter 7

Rudolf Steiner Foundation: The Art of Working Socially with Money

by

Siegfried Finser

In Germany, during the late 1960's, when a number of new Waldorf schools were being built every year, the impulse was born to work with capital in a more conscious way. Through the courage and insight of Wilhelm Ernst Barkoff, an attorney, and Gisela Reuther, subsequently the Treasurer of the General Anthroposophical Society, the first steps toward founding a bank based on the insights of Rudolf Steiner were taken. Rolf Kerler, currently the Treasurer of the General Anthroposophical Society, was the third person who made possible the start of the GLS Gemeinschaftbank EG.

Wilhelm Ernst Barkoff, Gisela Reuter and Rolf Kerler toured the main centers of Anthroposophy in North America in 1979, lecturing and bringing their important message to this country. We owe them all a great debt of appreciation for raising our consciousness and deepening our concerns about the forces inherent in the movement of money.

In 1983 the Rudolf Steiner Foundation began its work as a socially constructive financial service organization. As it grew and developed over the years, its legal form was found to be consistent with the newly emerging community loan fund movement. Increasingly, other mainstream foundations began to adjust their approaches, so that they are more like those of the Rudolf Steiner Foundation. The recent move to the Presidio in San Francisco placed the Foundation more directly into the mainstream of the philanthropic community in America.

The Role of the Foundation

From its beginning, the Foundation viewed the movement of money as a predominantly social phenomenon. It saw itself as a heart function in the continuous circulation of an enlivening stream of capital. Borrowers needed capital to fulfill their initiatives. Lenders needed the imaginations, intentions and initiatives of Borrowers to make their capital fruitful. Social leaders needed capital to provide the artistic, educational, spiritual and research functions of society for the refreshment and renewal of human capacities. Donors needed to connect with the social ideals of our culture to convert their personal karma into objective social good. Borrowers, Lenders, Givers and Receivers are interdependent in a stream of capital resources, flowing in a continuous lemniscate of financial and social health.

The Rudolf Steiner Foundation saw its role as the witness and facilitator, the servant of this fructifying movement of capital. Its task was to tend the various transactions between the Borrowers, Lenders, Donors and Receivers so that rightful relationships could flourish and so that the greatest amount of movement could take place unhampered.

By 1999 the total assets of the Rudolf Steiner Foundation totaled nearly $30 million. Of this total nearly $10 million are loaned to the Foundation by individuals, businesses and other not-for-profits. More than $12 million is loaned by the Foundation to socially constructive projects all over North America. In the course of the last fifteen years the Foundation has received more than $20 million in gifts and has directed nearly $17 million in gifts to charitable projects all over the world.

These numbers are modest compared to present needs and in light of future needs. Within the next ten years it is estimated that between $50 and $100 million in loans will be needed and even more than that in gifts to support the expansion of compatible, socially constructive projects, including the Waldorf schools.

Perhaps the most meaningful aspect of the Foundation's work is the possibility of pioneering social development through the vehicle of financing. The Rudolf Steiner Foundation has pioneered a variety of financial approaches that utilize the determined will and cooperative interworking of human beings to ensure repayment of loans, satisfy the requirements of collateral, and in the end optimize the potency of gifts. A brief description of some of these approaches is presented below.

The Support Community

If $400,000 is needed to complete a project, there are many ways of gathering this needed capital. Certainly one possibility which has often happened is that one or two wealthy people donate the entire amount. This produces the needed money quickly, with the least effort and, administratively, is least cumbersome and least expensive.

Another way is that 100 people each agree to provide the sum that is needed over a period of years. They may each pay differing amounts, but the average comes to $4,000. Over a 36 month period this requires monthly gifts of $112. If the same project united as many as 300 people, all determined to achieve the goal, the necessary contribution from each would be only $38 a month. The power of people working together in a determined way to achieve the same goal is a kind of social magic.

The fundamental posture of such an approach is that people are the most critical ingredient, not money. One doesn't raise money. Money does accumulate around a project, but only as a consequence of the people deciding what will happen. One looks for people, not money. The more people know of Waldorf education, appreciate it, the more the Waldorf schools will flourish. Money is only one necessary outcome—it usually comes as a result of the right climate and relationship among the people involved with the school: parents, teachers, children, friends.

For such a development to occur within the Waldorf school movement, the objective presence of a financial institution like the Rudolf Steiner Foundation is crucial to mediate between all the parties involved. The schools may be willing to help each other. The Foundation may then serve as objective witness of agreements and transactions between them. It protects the rights of each and, thereby, protects the rights of the whole without harm to the individual parts. The Foundation's role and presence as objective third party makes possible a greater degree of trust and cooperation between the schools.

Thus far, the concept of support community has been implemented locally, with some interest nationally and internationally, in a variety of projects, beginning with the Pine Hill Waldorf School. Perhaps the way it will grow will be project by project until an understanding of the basis of the fundamental social law grows and the practicality of its approach is demonstrated.

65

Subscription Pledge Agreements

In this country, a written promise to give a certain amount is not ordinarily a legally enforceable document. When, however an institution incurs a risk or expense in reliance upon such a promise, the document then becomes enforceable to the degree of any other contract. The Subscription Pledge Agreement has been developed by the Rudolf Steiner Foundation to enable a community of determined people to fund their project, if they are willing to promise to pay specific amounts for a specific amount of time. In reliance upon these Subscription Pledge Agreements, the Foundation will lend the school an amount equal to the sum total of all such agreements so that the facility can be built while the community repays the loan. Provisions are incorporated for the possible unexpected hardships of life and the potential for default.

Guarantee Agreements

To further enhance the working together of communities of people around the achievement of a project, the Foundation has made use of Guarantee Agreements to provide security for a loan. The money that is loaned to each project does not belong to the Foundation; it comes from people in the movement who have opened Lending Funds with the Foundation in order to provide funding for exactly such socially constructive projects. Any default would impact all of us, not just the wealthy, but many caring people who want the Waldorf school movement to continue to grow and are willing to lend their small savings for the sake of this ideal.

The close circle of parents and friends around a school borrowing money have to be prepared to absorb the inherent risk in such a project to protect the others who have provided the basic funding for the loan. They do this by signing Guarantee Agreements and depositing some percentage of the guarantied amount with the Foundation to back the guarantee. Once this group of friends take on the risk, they also acquire a heightened consciousness of the financial side of the project and are even more determined to make it a success.

Revolving Loan Association

In funding one project, for $1.2 million, all but the last $200,000 was able to be met in the repayment schedule. In order to carry this part of the total, a Revolving Loan Association was created. The Association issued 200 bonds, each with a face value of $1000.

New parents joining the school community were asked to purchase such a bond. When they left the school or their child graduated (in this case from Grade 8), their bond would become available for resale. In every case so far, the bond has been resold and the $1000 paid back if requested. The new owners of the bond are, of course, new parents joining the school. The bond pays interest to its owners, but this interest is agreed to be given to the school and helps reduce the cost.

In this way, about $200,000 of the building costs are always outstanding and are carried by the present parents of the school and by those to come. The Revolving Loan Association is a way to involve future parents in the creation of the basic and central facility of the school, by helping to carry its cost while enjoying its benefits.

A Spirit of Determined Cooperation

The basic ingredients of all these practical approaches are somewhat similar, building financial health and social achievement through forms that foster a spirit of determined cooperation. Together, the Foundation and the project depend on involving people in the school's development process, on building circles of friends and committed support groups. This not only accomplishes the objectives of a project, it also, and perhaps more importantly, creates the social context for serving the community in the right way. It takes the Waldorf school out of any insularity, out into the community that it serves.

The community around the project pledges gifts and/or signs guarantees that provide security for the Foundation's loan. This in turn provides meaning for the many individuals, businesses and other organizations that have loaned the funds to the Foundation. Giving and lending become meaningful social acts within the context of an array of projects, which foster socially constructive activity.

We can see from these approaches that working with money can be a social art. A financial institution for the Waldorf school movement cannot be a money machine. It, too, must be founded upon and strive for spiritual impulses, just as Waldorf education itself is charged with the spirit through and through.

With such thoughts at the core of its goals and activity, the Rudolf Steiner Foundation offers opportunities to begin working in this way. It permits people, non-profits, businesses and other organizations to give their surplus funds a deeper social meaning. Even $1000 dollars in a Lenders Fund of the Foundation can help support a Waldorf school's project. With a Lenders Fund, a particular project can be designated, or fields of interest selected, or even provide funding for the entire portfolio of projects. There are creditworthy projects in need of funding right now, and hopefully there will always be more. The Foundation foresees the need for more than $10 million to fund exciting projects now being developed in 1999 alone.

The Rudolf Steiner Foundation has worked closely with bringing about projects at many schools in North America, including New Hampshire, Massachusetts, Washington D. C., State of Washington, California, Colorado and many others, also in Canada. The Foundation also works cooperatively with compatible banking initiatives in other countries such as the GLS Gemeinschaftsbank E.G. (Germany), Mercury Provident Society (England), the Triodos Bank (Holland), and the Freie Gemeinschaftsbank (Switzerland). There are also financially oriented initiatives in this country, such as the Midwest Economic Group, which work socially with the insights of Rudolf Steiner and are compatible with the aims of the Rudolf Steiner Foundation.

Any Waldorf school contemplating a new building, purchase of property, or other project might wish to begin the process of establishing a relationship with the Foundation by keeping the Foundation's co-workers informed of its plans and activities. The earlier this is done, the better it is. The Foundation cannot deal with last minute requests. Its responsibility to the clients and their trust prohibits any rash or less than thoroughly researched loans.

Any Donor or individual contemplating a regular or periodic giving program can utilize the services of the Foundation which tries to honor the intentions of the donor while providing sound management and compliant processing of a variety of gift vehicles.

A Word of Caution

None of the ideas and examples described above is easy to implement, nor do any of them work prescriptively. The descriptions given here are an overview and should not be construed as a manual for do-it-yourself financing. Every project has its own dynamics and challenges and calls for unique approaches. Rarely can a solution used at one school be applied to another without going through the rigorous disciplines of fact gathering and creative financial structuring that is part of every project. On occasion one or another idea has been taken up and improperly implemented with a less than desirable result. This is usually due to the lack of involvement by the Foundation or a similar financial organization that can provide the necessary objectivity and experience. In the realm of finance, laws and forces are at work that cannot be overlooked without endangering even a well-intentioned project. Part of the challenge is to enter the reality of each situation with both courage and wisdom.

For copies of newsletters, annual reports or information about how to participate in financing the Waldorf school movement with interest bearing loans, address your request to:

The Rudolf Steiner Foundation
BLDG. 1002 B, Thoreau Ctr., Presidio
P. O. Box 29915
San Francisco, CA 94129-0915

telephone (415) 561-3900
FAX (415) 561-3919
E-mail: <mail@rsfoundation.org>

Chapter 8

Servant Leadership in Waldorf Schools

by

Bill Bottum and Dorothy Lenz

Rudolf Steiner and Robert Greenleaf were men many years ahead of their time. Though neither one knew nor read the other, their ideas are amazingly consonant and resonate harmoniously. This article is an invitation for you to contemplate what new possibilities could emerge from this fact.

Because readers of this handbook are very familiar with the life and work of Rudolf Steiner, let us begin with some information about Robert Greenleaf.

Greenleaf (1904-1990) was a teacher and consultant to universities and other corporations, for 40 years an executive at AT&T, and a lifelong student of how organizations work. In 1970, he coined the phrase "The Servant as Leader" in his essay published under that title. This gave a name and emphasis to his belief that the most effective leaders of the future will be first of all servants, not motivated by greed, selfishness, or the power to exploit, but by the desire to serve their fellow human beings. Greenleaf said that the best test of the servant as leader is "do those served grow as persons; do they, *while being served,* become healthier, wiser, freer, more autonomous, more themselves likely to become servants?" And, "what will be the effect on the least privileged in society? Will she or he benefit, or at least not be further deprived?"

In his 1980 essay "Servant: Retrospect and Prospect," Greenleaf spoke of "liberating visions which can come from anywhere," and added, "Important to me are:

• Immerse oneself in the experiences this world offers.

- Be accepting of the people involved in these experiences, and seek to understand what moves them.
- Acknowledge—stand in awe before—the ineffable mystery that shrouds the source of all understanding of human motives that leads to visions.
- Be open to receive, and act upon, what inspiration offers.

Greenleaf wrote many essays and lectured often on servant as leader, with the hope of encouraging thought which would lead to the development of a caring society through well managed institutions (what he called "the building blocks of society")—corporation, school, church, hospital, social agency, government. Interestingly enough, it is in a departure from his usual style of writing that Greenleaf was able to collect all of his ideas on servant as leader, with detailed examples, into one volume: his only fiction work, *Teacher as Servant - A Parable*, published in 1979. This was his personal favorite of all his writings—as well it might be. It is a masterpiece of teaching on many levels, academic material which touches the reader not only intellectually but deep within the soul. The very fact that this story is itself labeled as a parable indicates its teaching style and the style of teaching preferred by Greenleaf.

The plot is simple. A young man entering a university tells his own story. After answering a notice on a university bulletin board, "Do You Want To Be A Servant?," he finds himself living in Jefferson House, a unique dorm, the motto of which is "serve and be served." The headmaster is "an extraordinary one who dreamed a great dream of how servanthood could be nurtured in the young, and spent his best years bringing it to pass." The university allows but does not sponsor Jefferson House.

Greenleaf uses every aspect of the Jefferson House program to put across his own ideas about servant as leader—the way the House is managed, the way the headmaster guides, the way the students learn to answer their own questions. Special features of the program of the House, such as guest speakers, summer service jobs required of all students, House projects, continuous questioning and redefining of goals, and journaling by each student give Greenleaf specific avenues for outlining his own ideas and, in the process, demonstrating their efficacy. Speeches of two guests are printed verbatim; four complete reports by students are included (summer experiences being servants as leaders in a church, a school for leadership, a foundation-supported aid program in Africa, and an independent secondary school); a long-term House project, initiated by the narrating student, on improving the university's Board of Trustees, is described in detail, as is the youngman's experience of working after graduation in a company which is based on servant as leader; questions and journal entries abound.

The effect of all this is that the reader actually experiences for him/herself being servant as leader, ultimately coming to know, as intimately as possible short of actually being servant as leader, its process, its problems, and its triumphs.

Those seeking information generally spurn fiction, preferring to read straight forward accounts in the belief that this is the most expedient way to get to the heart of their subject. In this case, however, it is the reverse that is true. Though all of Greenleaf's works are well written, this parable is his most vivid and all-inclusive presentation of servant as leader, as well as being in itself a unique learning opportunity. Greenleaf said that he had put his heart and soul into this book and so was disappointed to find it the least popular of his writings. He would be pleased to know that just recently there has been a brisk upsurge of interest in *Teacher As Servant* among those who are serious about putting these principles to work in the institutions with which they are connected.

At this writing, two experimental models of Jefferson House have been in place for several years - Leadership House at the University of South Florida, in Tampa, and Hampton House at Butler University, in Indianapolis. These experiments in the real world are proving as successful as their fictional paradigm. Leadership House gained national attention at a leadership conference attended by delegates from all over the United States, and Hampton House was given the Program of the Year Award by the Great Lakes Association on Housing and Offices.

I have been studying Rudolf Steiner's three-folding ideas and experimenting with them in the business world for over 30 years and also studying and experimenting for 20 years with Greenleaf's idea of servant as leader.

The business world was extremely hostile to the thoughts of both of these men until a change began to occur at about the hundredth anniversary of the start of the Michaelic Age (1979). A recent study by Paul Ray, for the Fetzer Institute and Institute for Noetic Sciences, shows that now 25% of our adult population could be described as "cultural creatives," people suddenly more ready and open to ideas, similar to those of Steiner and Greenleaf, for bringing about cultural and spiritual

73

change. It is encouraging and exciting to observe and experience this Michaelic spirit beginning to manifest itself.

In the second chapter of his book, *Servant Leadership*, Bob Greenleaf describes the organizational form he thought most conducive to servant as leader. He called it a Council of Equals, facilitated by a primus inter pares (first among equals). In our construction company, we began to experiment with this in 1984, each of our 12 subsidiaries being represented on the Council. When I called Bob for a list of the companies who had tried such a Council, so we could compare notes, he said, "There aren't any." Today many organizations are using Greenleaf's Council of Equals, and manuals are written on how to employ such a concept. Some keys to an effective Council are mutual trust, openness, integrity, and empathetic listening. If only we had known in 1984 that Rudolf Steiner had already laid out the framework for the College of Teachers (very similar to the Council of Equals) and how it would operate, and that the Waldorf schools had been for over half a century successfully using this concept! Steiner, for example, had worked out the consensus decision making and the delicate relationship between the College of Teachers and the Board of Trustees.

In describing his ideas for setting up a three-fold society, Steiner suggests unbundling the economic sphere (based on fraternity), the political sphere (based on equality), and the spiritual/educational sphere (based on liberty). The three spheres would work together interdependently but be semi-independent, rather than locked together under the domination of the economic sphere as they are now. It would seem to me that Greenleaf's Council of Equals could prove a valuable contribution to this endeavor.

Greenleaf's belief that conflict resolution should be based on persuasion, empathetic listening, seeking and learning together, making room for collective and individual spirit to move within, and consensus, rather than anger, competition, argumentation and bullying is exactly the way that Steiner had envisioned the characteristics of all effective organizations.

Steiner's ideas turned the conventional wisdom of organization and governance upside down and inside out, replacing competitive "survival of the fittest" with collaboration, alliances among producers, suppliers, and consumers, in what we would call today a team-building relationship based on mutual interest and mutual trust.

In our construction company we applied this principle of collaboration to the relation between design engineers and constructors, whereas the conventional wisdom had thought it healthier to be always at each other's throats. Each time we used these team-building ideas, they turned the project around, and it was successful.

It is exciting to see how Greenleaf's concepts fit the spirit of Waldorf education and Steiner's interpretation of "liberty, equality, fraternity" in emphasizing the need for a new kind of leadership to meet effectively the challenges of our times. It is intriguing to ponder how their ideas could support each other in such ways as to create new pathways leading toward the fulfillment of the dream they both had for a world vibrant with dialogue and cooperation, rather than devastated by conflict.

Using the main character and narrator in *Teacher As Servant* as a mouthpiece for his own ideas, Greenleaf writes in the Prologue to the Parable, "For anything new to emerge there must first be a dream, an imaginative view of what might be. For something great to happen, there must be a great dream. Then venturesome persons with faith in that dream will persevere to bring it to reality. Some ideas whose time has come will spread as in a forest fire. But most need the help of a teacher."

Chapter 9

Alumni

by

Lou Rossi, PhD.

Once a Waldorf school is beyond its founding years it, begins to take a more active interest in its alumni body. Correspondingly, most alumni carry an interest in and a desire to stay in touch with their school. As time passes, interest in alumni from the school's side usually increases. They are recipients of the education, and the schools in many ways have helped shape their lives. As the alumni body gets larger and older, there is a desire find out how they are faring in life and to gather their thoughts and feelings about the education they received and how it affected their lives. They received a unique education and carry the fruits of that experience with them throughout their lives. On the other hand, alumni interest in their school may dissipate with time, unless the school takes the initiative to reach out in ways that will nurture in them a sense of belonging to the school community. The strong community life experienced in Waldorf schools provides a basis for life-long relationships with alumni to form.

Waldorf schools in North America are becoming more interested in their alumni. This is occurring both at individual schools and at the Association level as well. This writing will focus on organizing to develop meaningful alumni relations and to increase the involvement of alumni in the life of the school. The material for this article is drawn primarily from the author's experience with alumni relations over a two-decade period at High Mowing School, a 9th through12th Waldorf boarding-day school, in Wilton, New Hampshire. What follows applies directly to high school alumni. Elementary schools represent a different situation regarding their alumni that may well require a different approach. Adults, in general, carry a much stronger connection to the adolescent years of their youth in comparison to the elementary school years. Those memories form a cornerstone to relation building. For the elementary school alumni other factors may have to be called into play. Hopefully, what follows will encourage dialogue within your school community that will result in more clearly defined alumni policies and programs that will benefit the school and its alumni.

Where to start?

When a school becomes interested in formally reaching out to the alumni, it should create a simple statement of policy that defines the desired relationship with its alumni. The Development Committee (or equivalent group in your school) should propose the alumni policy statement to the governing body. The policy statement should state the importance of alumni inclusion in the community and lend support and direction to programs that would productively include alumni in the school process. The approved policy will serve as a guide for the faculty, administrators, trustees, staff, and the operating committees. A task for the Development Committee would be to update the policy periodically and to recommend alumni programs and practices to the governing body that are consistent with the policy, as well as the more practical school considerations of school budgeting, staffing, and program.

The Role of the Development Committee (or Equivalent Body)

For purposes of this article it will be assumed that the school's Development Committee oversees all the community relations and fund raising programs for the school. With the approval of the governing body, it will set development goals, objectives, and policies and oversees the work of the paid development staff. Depending on the school, it is understood that the development function could be delegated differently; this should not affect the process described herein. The committee operates as an arm of the governing body at the school and consists of representatives of the faculty, staff, trustees and other community members. Among its tasks, the Development Committee will be responsible for overseeing all alumni affairs within the school community.

The types of activities that a school, through the Development Committee and staff, can consider for the involvement of its alumni include:

- Involvement with community events, plays, fairs, auctions, graduation, etc., with either their attendance or involvement with implementation.

- Volunteering in the classroom:
    Teaching a high school main lesson
    Giving classroom presentations (where their career or life experience can add real insight to a classroom subject)
    As artisans to work along side students in the arts and crafts studios, coaching athletic teams

- Volunteering in the library. (Students, in particular, welcome opportunities to meet and talk with alumni.)

- Volunteering in administration:
    To join open houses for admissions. Prospective parents find it helpful to communicate with selected alumni of the school.
    To serve on operating committees where talent and expertise can be put to use.
    To serve as trustees, either for expertise or to represent the alumni body.

- Participating in alumni surveys—a great way to get to know what your alumni are up to and how they feel about the school.

- In faculty positions. Alumni who pursue teaching careers often train as Waldorf teachers.

- As parents in Waldorf schools.

- Participating in school community building and maintenance projects

- Participating in Annual Giving and other fund-raising projects.

- Writing articles for the school newsletter.

To successfully and productively incorporate alumni into school programs and activities, the results must be helpful to the school and satisfying for the volunteer. This is where the development staff is important. They should know the alumni volunteer as they do the parent volunteer, and a good match between an individual's interest and skill level and the project at hand is a vital ingredient for success.

Another important function of the Development Committee is to oversee the work of the development staff in Alumni relations. This includes:

Maintaining the database

At least alumni addresses, phone numbers (e-mail addresses and fax numbers as appropriate), years at school and graduation year, and gift records should be maintained. As people are on the move, it is useful today to obtain social security numbers, which can be used to track lost addresses. As the organization and level of sophistication grow, additional information can be accumulated, such as personal and professional interests, school contacts, career information, birth dates, family information, etc. As the alumni body enlarges, an alumni directory can be published.

Including alumni in your database is very easy. Keeping updated files involves effort and budgeting. Without it, the alumni community will become weak and fragmented.

Recognition

Individuals must be recognized for their efforts and other contributions within the context of the school community. Proper recognition validates the importance that the school attaches to its community members individually and as a group. This includes gift and volunteer service acknowledgments and a thank you, alumni achievements that can be on display at the school, articles about alumni in the school newsletter, etc.

Provide Links to Classmates and Former Faculty

Classmates, faculty, and the school environment (physical things like location, buildings, scenery) are what alumni first recall when thinking of their school experience. Among the first thoughts are, "Where is Jane Smith now and what is she doing?" Responding to this type of inquiry is key to including alumni as active and productive community members.

Opportunities abound to reconnect alumni with classmates and teachers, and in the process they become stronger community members with deeper connections to the school. Send special invitations to school functions and events to all alumni; graduation, fairs, auctions, performances, etc. Attending school events becomes an opportunity to visit old friends and to draw closer to the school process. Even if alumni do not attend, the invitation confirms that they are members of the community and welcomed at the school.

Schools with larger alumni bodies can have alumni gatherings in larger metropolitan areas. One or two alumni in the city who will organize and host the event with staff support from the school to generally help set these up. The faculty chair and a selected faculty member or two will represent the school.

Alumni reunions at the school are popular and well attended. Certain anniversary years seem to draw the most alumni; they are the 5-, 10-, 20-, 25 and 30-year reunions. There are a few Waldorf schools that have held 50-year reunions.

Communications

The school newsletter will be the periodical communication that the alumni will receive from the school.

They should also receive brochures, annual giving appeals, invitations to school events, etc. In the newsletter consider including a section on personal notes received from alumni and printed by class as well as articles about alumni articles. Alumni often write to the school or faculty describing something of their current lives. Collect, edit and print them up in your newsletter. Once started, the information will flow, and there will be plenty to write about. With e-mail and the Internet, the school can become a real center for alumni communications. More established schools will publish an alumni newsletter and an alumni directory.

School displays on the alumni works, newspaper clippings, public recognition, etc. help everyone learn more about your alumni. We keep on display in the library books authored by our alumni.

Organizing for Larger Alumni Bodies

There are a number of factors that determine when the Development Committee will move in the direction of establishing an Alumni Association and Class Representatives. The factors to consider include support staff cost; the number and age span of the alumni, and the degree in which alumni are incorporated into the life of the school. If a school has an alumni population exceeding 500 with the oldest in their 50's, they are ready to consider an Alumni Association and class representatives.

Class Representatives

Volunteer Class Reps will assist the school and the alumni in maintaining class identity, communications within the class, communications between the class and school, and an up-dated database of addresses. In most cases Class Reps will also phone class members for annual giving solicitation. When your best Class Rep candidate doesn't like to ask for gift money, someone else in the class can be asked to perform that duty.

Within the development staff, the individual in charge of alumni (the Alumni Director) will recruit a Class Representative for each class. The Alumni Director will prepare a Class Representative job description which outlines the duties and responsibilities to perform the above listed functions. Letter, phone, or e-mail accomplish communications between the reps and classmates. Information that passes hands includes personal notes for publication in the newsletter, address updates, whereabouts of lost alumni, school news and events of note, encouragement to visit the school, and planning class reunions.

The Alumni Director must keep in periodic contact with the class representatives.

The Alumni Association

The Association is a body whose function it is promote communications between the school and the alumni and within the alumni body. Organizationally, it is an arm of the Development Committee. At our school, all alumni belong to the Association and a small group of alumni are appointed by the Alumni Director to form the Association Council, which nominates officers (for election at the Association annual meeting at Alumni Weekend) and conducts its meetings, including the annual meeting.

The Council appoints the alumni representatives to the trustees. The Council oversees the class rep network along with the Alumni Director and plans activities in support of the school and the alumni presence in the school.

Annual Giving and the Alumni

As a school reaches out to its alumni and involves them, Annual Giving will begin to take hold in a meaningful way. Giving becomes an integral part of the relationship between the school and its alumni body.

The Development Committee conducts the process that approves the giving goals and solicitation program for the alumni. The alumni leadership at the school (trustees, council members, etc.,) should be part of the process.

The importance of alumni participation in Annual Giving cannot be overstressed. Participation in annual giving builds towards the future. The major donors of tomorrow will come from the small donors of today.

More importantly, young alumni will become disenfranchised, if they feel that their small gift is not appreciated.

The ultimate goal should be alumni soliciting their classmates for Annual Giving. A sound annual giving program will set the stage for the future involvement of alumni in Capital and Planned Giving. There is much to be said about Annual Giving and the alumni which can be a future article.

Some Frequently Asked Questions

When do you begin communicating with young graduates as alumni?

During the middle of their senior year, students will begin focusing on life beyond high school. It is towards the end of the senior year that life as an alumnus of the school can be addressed to the class. At High Mowing we have a senior dinner sponsored by the school and the Alumni Council. The conversation following dinner ranges from the importance of participation in Annual Giving (give a dollar for each year out of school) to informing the school of address changes. They are encouraged to return to school often and to come back for alumni weekend. Our alumni weekend follows graduation, and we have selected juniors and seniors on hand to talk with alumni about the school today.

Students who attended our school for a short period of time— should they be included as alumni?

The simple answer is yes, and let them decide the relationship for themselves. Some will stay as community members, and others will ask to be removed from the mailing list. We have a good number of individuals who are participating alumni that never graduated, even ones that were expelled. You can never predict the outcome with those who didn't graduate. It is best to let them decide and accept them as full members of the alumni body.

How about Elementary Schools and their Alumni?

If an independent school ends at grade 8 or lower, it is generally accepted to be more difficult to cultivate alumni relations. Individuals have a more vivid recollection of their high school years. I often find our alumni attach more significance to their High Mowing years than to their college years.

Waldorf elementary schools may attract the interest of alumni owing to the strong community life fostered at our schools and to the uniqueness of the curriculum. I have little experience with alumni at the elementary school level and leave the question to be addressed by someone who does.

Include Alumni as Part of your Community

The notion of alumni belonging to the school community is obvious; however, in practice it can generate mixed results unless the school alumni policy is clear and understood by the school faculty and administrators. Good intentions will only go so far, and an example will make the point. One alumna who is productively involved with our school today recalls an incident that occurred to her at High Mowing. She was returning to the school for the first time, some 15 years after graduation. She recalled a friendly environment, but she felt no connection to most of the faculty at the time. To her it was the school of her youth that she loved and cherished, yet no one seemed to pay any attention to her or her family members. To the faculty and staff she felt like a stranger, "As though I was someone who found their way onto the campus following a wrong turn off the highway." She was received with questions the equivalent of, "Who are you?" and, "What are you doing here?" She felt isolated and unwanted, even though alumni were welcome at the school. Written policies and practices that are well communicated and accepted throughout the community are a good place to start, if good intentions towards alumni are to be carried out in practice.

Alumni carry warm feelings towards their school experience and will appreciate the opportunity to remain connected to the school throughout their lives. It remains for the school to define the relationship with the alumni and to clearly communicate alumni relations policy to the entire community.

Chapter 10

The Role of Gift Money in a Waldorf School

by

Martin Novom, CFRE

The premise of this article is that the value of encouraging and obtaining gift support for a Waldorf school goes far beyond just cash income. Many schools have benefitted and continue to benefit greatly from a flow of charitable gifts. However, if the desire for increased cash flow remains the main rationale behind our efforts to seek gifts, our schools can miss some rather significant organizational and human growth opportunities. I hope that this article will encourage you to not only seek philanthropic support in your school but also to broaden your thinking about why you do it. As a student of the mysteries of gift money, I think about it a great deal.

Having been fortunate to work with Waldorf schools in almost every region of the country, I can report that we have made very long strides in increasing the flow of gift money. We have also improved the degree to which we highlight the contributions of trustees, volunteers and donors in their efforts to support the mission of their school. The importance of professionalizing our philanthropic support efforts and investing appropriate amounts of precious staff resources to do so has become more and more evident. The number of schools utilizing annual giving, major gift programs, and capital campaigns has increased dramatically in just the last seven years.

All of this growth seems to parallel a decrease in the stigma surrounding money and about charitable gifts in particular. It appears that we have learned a great deal from the long established independent schools and from nonprofit organizations in general. I hope this is encouraging to those of you who feel drawn to focus on philanthropic support programs in your school. We have a great deal more we can learn from other nonprofit organizations. To do so we will have to be constantly in touch with our nonprofit counterparts, analyzing what they are doing (and why) and being willing to draw lessons from them, experimenting and adapting what we've learned for our individual school and our locale.

To limit our search to only those ideas external to our school is, I believe, a great mistake. We can learn a quite a bit from observing our own school community, its behaviors, its programs and how our people react to them. I hope you will join me and the growing ranks of others that are willing to think "outside the box" on this issue.

With that as an introduction, allow me to outline what I feel are some important benefits to our schools from the pursuit of philanthropic support, and, therefore, some potential rationale beyond just increasing the cash flow. This is just a start, and I urge you to add your observations and points to the list of possible benefits.

Some Definitions

Since I use a few terms, its important to offer some definitions. Philanthropy is bigger than fund development and much broader than fundraising. Here is how.

Fundraising is seeking donations from various sources for the support of an organization or a specific project.

Fund development is the planning and implementing of programs that are meant to increase contributed financial support for an organization.

Philanthropy includes the worlds of:
        donated money
        donated time
        mandated activity in association with others.

Philanthropic support programs would be those that seek to identify, foster and promote, monitor and evaluate the growth and health of a continuous flow of prospective donors, current donors, past donors, volunteers or trustees. You can see why I prefer the word philanthropy to the phrase fundraising.

Gift Money as a Lightning Rod for Issues

Ask anyone who has tried to plan or launch a capital campaign. As soon as you begin asking for serious sums of gift money, any issues individuals are carrying get placed right out on the table fast. Since capital campaigns involve what can be called sacrificial levels of giving, they are wonderful in that way.

Regardless of the size or type of philanthropic program you can count on it being very effective at getting to the heart of any issue or dispute living in the individuals in your school. It can be particularly helpful when issues are generally known to exist, but solutions have been illusive or too painful to implement. When a significant program or building is believed to be important to the growth of the school, it can create a climate that focuses enough attention so that an otherwise painful or difficult issue gets placed at the top of the agenda.

I am aware of the risk that just because a project is being discussed the need to attract gift money can be misused and become a platform for partisanship. I work under the assumption that healthy philanthropic support programs happen when gift supported projects are considered, authorized and conducted by fully informed participants under properly mandated and evaluated processes.

The Pursuit of Gifts Can Clarify Goals

How often have we experienced well-meaning friends of the school ready to create programs to raise money without the least semblance of a set of goals as to why we need the money? Let's have an auction! Let's have a capital campaign! While I could use this an opportunity to advocate for the value of planning, suffice it say that the most money gets raised, the most volunteers become involved (and find satisfaction) and the greatest opportunities for volunteer leadership and growth happen when there are plans based on clear and widely supported goals.

Unfortunately, any form of planning (long range planning, strategic planning, future search, etc.) is not usually high on the list of everyone's favorite activity. Planning in any form is likely to be overlooked in the rush to fund school growth. Isn't it great then that the pursuit of philanthropic support gives us the opportunity to get our goals sorted out? Said another way, we really can't be successful in raising funds or increasing the number of our school's friends if we don't have clear goals that have wide support.

An Arena in Which Leadership Grows

Finding individuals with leadership skills is difficult in all areas of modern life, be it commerce, public service or culture. Our Waldorf schools are also challenged in trying to identify and encourage the expression and growth of leadership for our group and individual work. The scope of this article is primarily focused on volunteer, governance and administrative activity and not on the arena of pedagogy or the work of the Faculty. However, leadership opportunities stemming from involvement in the creation and oversight of philanthropic support programs can be a wonderful group learning process for any adult in the school. Observers of philanthropic support processes report that the intensive nature of delegated and evaluated activity practically demands that the best practices of group work and human interaction sensitivity be employed. Said another way, if you want to successfully raise friends and money for your school, you will find yourself practically forced to pinpoint, adopt and evaluate what it means to take initiative and allow others to do so in group work. As we would expect, how each school does it is a reflection of the ethos of that particular school.

A Focal Point for Advocacy of the School

Whether we are thinking about strengthening and retaining enrollment or building and maintaining a flow of philanthropic support, advocacy for the school is a natural byproduct. Here's why. In order for a philanthropic program to be successful, all solicitations for funds or personal involvement from others require that the volunteer asking creates and adopts their own rationale for gift or volunteer support. "How can I ask another person to make a gift, or to volunteer, if I am not clear why the school is important to me?" Often we don't make this connection until we are in a major gift or capital campaign solicitation. When we are preparing volunteer solicitors, we encourage them to make their pledge or gift before they go out and ask another prospective donor. Why? We know that just the process of being asked prepares a solicitor by having to face inwardly just how they feel about the school. Once having made the decision to make a pledge or gift, the volunteer solicitor is usually much clearer on why the school and the particular project is important to them. The bottom line here is that philanthropic support programs almost force us to engage in an inner dialogue about our feelings about the school. Then it helps us by setting up a context around which we formulate language for our feelings. This is training in advocacy skills!

Balancing the Pressure from Heavy Reliance on Tuition

The pursuit of philanthropic support can have an enlivening effect on what is sometimes felt as the deadening financial burden of tuition. Many of the parents in our schools did not attend private school, and, therefore, the choice of Waldorf education often has a powerful financial impact on the families of the school.

Without the option of charitable gifts as an income source, the school budget can only place ever-greater upward pressure on tuition. A school with little or no charitable gifts is likely to suffer from one or both of these: a) an overworked and/or underpaid faculty susceptible over time to high turnover; b) a population moving over time to fewer and fewer families with moderate incomes.

Depending on how any school chooses to employ philanthropic support, there can arise an explicit or implicit linkage with the concept of less than total reliance on tuition. It would be improper, if not just guesswork, for me to say what is appropriate in any one situation. Clearly, though, this an area ripe for further dialogue.

Looking Ahead

Let me conclude by "raising the bar" of our expectations, and I don't mean aspiring to higher levels of gift support. I think we should give serious consideration as to whether it is satisfactory any longer for us to just raise gift support for its own sake.

Are we taking full measure of what we have before us as the complete school community? Can we afford any longer to not see the entire range of personal and organizational growth opportunities for all adults, not just those who are faculty and staff?

What's that you say? "We don't have room in our entirely too full school agenda to involve trustees and other volunteers in anything more than just getting the work done," someone might say. I see a direction where the work not only gets done, but it involves trustees and volunteers in such a way that they form stronger links with the school, feel more fulfilled by helping the school attain its goals, and find they have grown in their ability to do meaningful work and, perhaps even, develop some leadership skills. The direction I have in mind is fully conscious, mandated and evaluated philanthropic support programs. Best of all, if it is done with the right attitude, it can include large doses of joy. Joyful philanthropy, now that's a worthy goal.

Chapter 11

Fund Development/Philanthropic Support

by

Kay Skonieczny and David Mitchell

It is important from the very beginning for a Waldorf school to consistently cultivate an environment where generosity is encouraged, nurtured and acknowledged. Those who have taken on leadership roles in the school need to model the generosity, involvement and understanding the school is looking for from its circle of parents, alumni and friends.

Gifts of time, expertise and dollars are gladly and generously given when individuals feel involved and a valued part of the community and when there is respect, trust and confidence in the school's pedagogical, administrative and financial stability. Gift giving works in concentric circles and must begin with those closest to the school (Board, faculty, staff, parents) and spread outward to alumni, alumni parents, grandparents, friends, and then to corporations and foundations.

The 90% factor in philanthropy is the individual, since 90% of the money contributed to charities comes from the individual donor; 5% comes from corporations and 5% from foundations. Keep this in mind when setting the goals and priorities for the school's fund development efforts. Fund development includes Annual Giving, capital campaigns, planned giving, grant writing and special events. This chapter will address Annual Giving, capital campaigns, grant writing and special events.

Annual Giving

The Annual Giving Campaign is the foundation of your fund development program. Through this activity you build your base of support, draw out and nurture the capacity for generous giving.

The purpose of an Annual Gving Campaign is to:

- provide essential operating funds to carry out the mission of the school
- build and broaden the school's base of financial support
- give individuals the opportunity for involvement, education and commitment
- nurture the capacity for capital and planned gifts

The components for a successful Annual Campaign are:

- an ability to capture the imagination of individuals with your description of the school's vision, dreams, programs
- a school with an excellent faculty who are inclusive, inviting and inspiring
- a school that is well managed and has financial accountability
- a school where there is enthusiastic involvement and leadership of parents on committees, the Board, educational and social events
- a campaign plan that includes goals, leadership, volunteers, timelines, solicitation methods, recognition and evaluation
- a combination of methods of solicitation letter, phone and personal visits

The Annual Giving Campaign can sometimes become routine when it needs to be filled with passion and enthusiasm. Some questions to ask yourself about your campaign:

Does it communicate HOPE?
Does it talk about dreams as well as strategic plans?
Does it remind and re-inspire your donors why they were attracted to Waldorf education and/or your school in the first place?
Does it invite your donors to join with others to do more than they could alone; to become one with the universal circle of

those who share their goodness and goods for the benefit of many?

Create opportunities for everyone in the school community to renew their enthusiasm, their commitment to your school. Every meeting, gathering, event, performance is an opportunity for a conscious reminder. Bring stories from the classroom, parents' observations from home, artwork, etc. into the various meetings parents attend at the school. Begin the meeting with a simple song, a eurythmy gesture to enhance parents' experience of the education.

Use constant gratitude reminders on how the gifts to the Annual Campaign are making many things possible. For example, in your school newsletter, you could have a line that said: Funding for this newsletter is made possible by generous gifts to the Annual Giving Campaign. Say thank you to the parents (alumni, grandparents, friends) whose gifts to the Annual Giving Campaign made this lecture (parent workshop, library resource, faculty conference, etc.) possible. All school performances are also an opportunity to make a brief statement about the value of Waldorf education and the gratitude you have for those who make it possible (parents, Board members, teachers, staff, etc.) who give generously of their time and their financial resources.

Individuals may differ in how they want to be publicly acknowledged, but everyone likes to feel appreciated and to know that their gifts are making a difference in the life of the school.

Mailing Lists

An accurate mailing list is essential for a successful fund development program. It is important to maintain a current list of all those who are or have been associated with your school: parents, Board members, past parents, alumni, grandparents, faculty and staff. It is equally important to keep a list of people who inquire about the school, attend a school fair or lecture. This is a way to continually reach a broader audience for your school events, enrollment and parent education programs. To help you maintain accurate lists, consistently ask people in your newsletters and mailings to call or e-mail the school if they have a change of address or would like to have their name removed.

Community Outreach

Establish your school as a center for cultural and educational opportunities in your community. Such events could include festival celebrations, lectures, craft and art classes, concerts, folk or other popular dances. Whenever you sponsor a community event, be sure to have information on the school available, the children's work displayed and a sign-up sheet for your mailing list.

Communication

It is vitally important that the individuals on your annual giving mailing list hear from the school many times throughout the year. Take every opportunity to inform people of events and school news, ask for their input and thank them for their involvement and support. Find ways to keep in touch with alumni and alumni parents, a vital long term resource for the school.

Timing

The Annual Giving Campaign is conducted at most schools in the fall. What is most important is that the campaign occur at the same time each year. Donors come to expect the appeal and plan for their contribution at that time of the year. New parents need to know that gift money is an important part of the school's income streams and need to be encouraged to participate when given an opportunity.

Campaign Plan

Participation is a key element in annual giving. Schools strive for 100% participation, especially among the key leadership groups of Board, faculty, staff and committees. The campaign needs to have a dollar goal that is realistic and related to a few specific program needs. It should have a timeline, usually eight to twelve weeks, with a beginning and an end, so that it does not drag on throughout the school year. Donors can give a one time gift or make a pledge payable by the end of the school year. A letter or a brochure (or both) with a donor response envelope is sent to the school's mailing list. A select number of key individual donors may be asked personally for their gift. Follow up with a phonathon to call those who did not respond to the letter.

The letter and/or brochure should capture the imagination of the reader as well as inform of the school's needs and accomplishments. It is important to state that each gift, large or small, is needed, welcomed and appreciated. Many schools invite parents, Board members, alumni or alumni parents to write the letter. This can be very effective. It is also very helpful if some bit of student artwork or creative writing can be included in the letter or as a border or heading.

The reply envelope should give the donor options for type of payment (cash, credit card, securities). It should also ask for information that the school would like to know about the donor, such as current address, phone, and whether the donor is a parent, alum, past parent, etc. The reply envelope is a good place to ask individuals if they work for a company that gives matching gifts. Information on companies that match employee gifts can be obtained from CASE, the Council for Advancement and Support of Education, at Suite 400, 11 Dupont Circle, Washington, DC 20036. You can also plant a seed for planned giving by including a line about getting further information on including the school in the donor's will or estate plans. Be sure to print a big THANK YOU somewhere on the envelope.

Acknowledgment

Acknowledge each gift received as soon as possible. Keep accurate and up-to-date donor records. The number and size of gifts a donor makes can help to identify potential major contributors for capital and endowment campaigns.

A phonathon can be organized to follow up on individuals who did not respond to the initial appeal letter. Select a group of volunteers who will gather to make calls at the school or at a business that has several phone lines on one or more evenings. Publicize the phonathon in your newsletter and ask people who will be called to give a few minutes of their time to hear what the volunteer has to say. Provide a script as part of the training for the phonathon volunteers. The script should provide information about the Annual Campaign's goals and timelines. It should also include the most current information about the school's enrollment, financial stability and any new projects or programs. Prepare a donor record sheet on each person to be called that includes their giving history and what grades their children are in school. If it is an alum or past parent, it would be helpful to know when they or their children attended the school. Callers succeed when they can speak of their own commitment to the school and the campaign, invite the individual called to join with them, respond to an individual's questions or comments, and listen attentively.

Reporting/Evaluation

Report the progress of the campaign at regular intervals and at the conclusion of the campaign. Thank all those who participated and the volunteers who helped the campaign succeed. Find ways throughout the year to remind donors of how their annual giving dollars are supporting programs. Ask volunteers for feedback on what could be done to improve the campaign for the next year.

Capital Campaigns

A Capital Campaign provides funds for building and/or renovation projects and endowments. It is conducted over a specific period of time, usually six, nine or twelve months with a pledge payment period extending over a three to five year period. It requires a more generous level of giving to reach major dollar goals. Many times a project will be funded by a combination of a Capital Campaign, loans and reserved monies. It requires passion and persistence!

Schools often hire a consultant to assess the school's ability to raise capital funds and to coordinate the campaign. It should be noted that consultants do not raise the money for the school; they help the school present its project and organize its volunteers who will raise the money.

Capital campaigns require the following readiness factors:

- a defined need agreed upon by the majority of constituents and backed by a strong case for support
- a pool of donors/donor prospects with accurate, current information on these
- a team of enthusiastic volunteers willing to ask for gifts
- a leadership team able to inspire and attract support of major donors
- a realistic assessment of the potential for raising the dollar goal.

Capital Campaigns Require Structure

Determine a specific length of time for the campaign to be conducted (six to twelve months). Stick to it! Don't let the campaign drag on and on. The pledge payment period is usually extended beyond the campaign period for several years (three to five). Follow up during the pledge payment period is extremely important.

The usual structure for a campaign is a campaign chair, a campaign cabinet or steering committee, a major gifts committee, and captains and teams for various segments of the donor pool (parents, alumni, past parents, etc.). It is ideal if the campaign chair is someone inspiring, well known and able to give a leadership gift as well as solicit major gifts. Campaigns sometimes have honorary chairs who are well known and a campaign chair who is able to give leadership and attention to the cabinet or steering committee. Regular committee meetings, assignments and specified reporting dates are vital to success.

The major gifts committee selects and solicits the prospective donors who will be the 20% to provide 80% of the campaign goal. Pace setting, large gifts are important to be secured as early as possible to provide leadership and impetus for the campaign. Major gift prospects are asked for their gift face to face. This type of solicitation is most successful when a peer of the potential donor makes the appointment, shares his/her own commitment to the project and asks for a gift of a specific amount. Often a school or campaign representative accompanies the volunteer on the call to answer any questions about the school or the project.

Personal visits to as many campaign prospects as possible is a key factor in the success of capital campaigns. Phone calls are made to those who cannot be visited and a final letter solicitation is made to all other remaining prospects toward the end of the campaign.

It is important to decide early how donors will be recognized so that any special opportunities for recognition can be made known.

Capital Campaign Communication

Schools will want to utilize their regular avenues of communication but could add a regular "Campaign Progress Report" insert or a special "Campaign Column" in the school newsletter to give the campaign consistent exposure. The insert or column could state the most frequently asked questions about the project or the campaign and give the answers. It could thank those who have joined the campaign volunteers and recruit others.

Depending on the theme or timing of the campaign, it could coincide with a school anniversary or milestone. An annual special event could connect with the campaign, or the campaign could create its own kick-off or special event. General community publicity through the press or media is usually sought when the campaign is well underway with the campaign leadership in place and lead gifts secured.

Communication Pieces Typical for a Capital Campaign

A Case for Support document that describes the school's history, vision, plans, accomplishments, current needs and proposed project to meet the needs.

A campaign brochure, attractive and inspirational, that outlines the need, the proposed project and the campaign goal, timeline and gift levels.

A pledge card that provides the donor with various options for payment and records important data on the donor.

A letter from the campaign chair stating his/her own commitment to the project and encouraging others to join in investing in the school's future.

Campaign Records, Reports, Acknowledgments

A Capital Campaign payment period can last over several years, so it is very important to keep accurate records of gifts pledged, payments made and reminders sent. Donors are eager to hear of the project's progress; continue to report regularly. Thank you letters should be timely and attention and follow through given to any special ways donors are to be recognized.

Celebration

A Capital Campaign calls forth a great amount of energy and good will. It can foster a strong feeling of community accomplishment. The school has created an opportunity for individuals to renew their dedication to its vision and purpose and share of their personal resources to help realize a dream. This is a moment for blessing, thanksgiving, reflection, celebration for the whole community.

Samples of Annual and Capital Campaign Materials

The AWSNA office keeps a current file of letters, brochures, donor response cards, etc., used in campaigns at various Waldorf schools across North America. Please call the AWSNA Development Office if you would like further information.

Special Events

Special events that raise money include: auctions, fairs (Christmas, harvest, May Day), dinner dances and concerts. With the right leadership, planning and participation, an event could raise $20,000 to $50,000 or more.

In addition to raising money, special events are important in the life of a school for their social value, their community and team building efforts. Working together to ensure a successful event of high quality helps teachers, parents, Board members, past parents and alumni form friendship bonds that last a lifetime. These events are an opportunity for community outreach to increase the school's visibility and support enrollment activities.

Foundations

Finally, there are foundations which are sources from which schools can apply for funds.

A foundation is a nongovernmental, nonprofit organization with its own funds and programs managed by its own Board of Trustees. Foundations are established to aid educational, social, artistic, charitable, or other activities serving the common welfare primarily by making grants to other nonprofit organizations. Some foundations may use different words in their names, such as "fund," "endowment," or "trust," but these terms are not legally or operationally different. Education has always ranked highest on the list of beneficiaries of foundations.

Five Basic Kinds of Foundations

The **independent foundations** have assets which come from the gift of an individual or family who has decided how the foundation shall issue grants and to what specific purposes. These foundations are most frequently local in character and are the most important source. Two examples of large independent foundations are the Carnegie Corporation and the Ford Foundation.

The **company sponsored foundations** derive their assets from a profit making company or corporation, but are a separately constituted organization. Their giving tends to focus on the community where the corporation operates, in fields related to corporate activities or to nonprofit organizations connected with their employees. Many companies will match gifts given to Waldorf Schools by their employees. Digital and General Motors are two large companies with company sponsored foundations.

The **community foundations** are publicly supported organizations which derive their funds from many donors. Their grantmaking activities are generally limited to charitable organizations in their local communities. They are usually classified by the IRS as public charities and, therefore, are not subject to the same regulatory provisions that apply to private foundations. They are among the most open foundations, and they usually make a great deal of information available about their activities. The New York, San Francisco, and Cleveland Foundations are three of the largest of the approximately 250 community foundations.

The **Federal Government** operates several programs with similarities to foundations. They are funded from tax monies appropriated by Congress, and they function as government agencies rather than as private foundations. Examples include the National Endowment for the Arts and the National Science Foundation.

Operating foundations also maintain a fund derived from a single source, but their primary purpose is to operate research, social welfare, or other programs determined by their governing body. They generally make few if any grants to other organizations. The Twentieth Century Fund and the Amherst H. Wilder Foundation are examples of operating foundations.

Each year nearly one million requests for funding are made to the approximately 22,000 active foundations in the United States. Of these requests, perhaps no more than six or seven percent eventually obtain the support they were seeking.

The vast majority of these requests are declined, some because there are never enough funds to go around, but many because they represent programs which do not match the guidelines of the foundation. Grant requests may also be denied because the applications are poorly prepared and do not reflect a careful analysis of the organization's needs or its capacity to carry out the program proposed.

Each foundation is unique, and you should be sure to find out about the selection process demanded by the particular foundation that you have applied to. The improper solicitation of a foundation can damage your reputation and can harm other Waldorf schools as well!

To assist in researching for proposal writing, the foundations in North America have created The Foundation Center to assist in the soliciting of grants. The Foundation Center is a resource center whose purpose is to assist in the proper application for grants.

Information can be received by writing to:

The Foundation Center
79 Fifth Avenue
New York, NY 10003

or

The Foundation Center
312 Sutter Street, Suite 312
San Francisco, CA 94108
Telephone 415-397-0903
www.fdncenter.org

Unlike other funding sources foundations do not issue lists or announcements specifying available grants. The best indication of their current interests is for you to research their recent funding patterns. The Foundation Center published COMSEARCH which is made up of printouts of all actual grants made of $5,000 or more to non-profit institutions.

Many foundations place limits on their giving, including subject areas, recipient types, and geographic locations. Finding out about these limitations before you submit your proposal will save you a great deal of time.

After developing a list of foundations with a funding history in your field, you must learn as much as possible about each. Such information is available in annual reports published by approximately 500 foundations. The IRS publishes tax returns for all private foundations—these can be found in the following Foundation Center's resources:

National Data Book (an analysis of grantmaking by assets, grants, type and state);

Corporate Foundation Profiles (detailed analysis of the 230 largest, company sponsored foundations plus a brief profile of an additional 400 corporate foundations, the fastest growing segment of the foundation community);

Guide To Foundation Profiles (covers 711 companies, listing significant information and a statistical analysis);

Source Book Files (This comes out quarterly and provides a 4-8 page analysis of the 1,000 largest foundations. This book breaks each grant down into area of giving, type of grant, support awarded, and types of recipient organizations).

The Foundation Center recommends strict adherence to the following questions:

1. Does the foundation have any geographic limitations which would disqualify your proposal?

101

2. Does your project or organization fall within the foundations stated or traditional giving program?

3. Does the foundation make grants for the type of support you need? (construction, science supplies operating budget, etc.)

4. Does the foundation make grants in the amount that you need?

5. Does the foundation have particular application guidelines or procedures to be followed and have you followed them?

Schools should cultivate both big and small foundations in their own geographical area. If you determine that the grantmaking interests of a foundation in your own community coincide with those of your school, you will want to create a good relationship with the appropriate staff members. It might be possible to build a funding structure using a variety of components. For example, you could solicit small grants, from $150-$6,000, from local foundations for continuing support and only approach the large foundations when you have a large project.

Even after you have properly researched and identified the foundations who receive your proposal, you are not prepared to write your grant. First, you will have to examine if the foundation has any set procedures or steps that must be followed. Many foundations have no applications and leave the grantseeker free to present their ideas in the most appropriate format. However, all foundations do expect to find certain facts and figures in all proposals that they receive. The following is a checklist of what a good proposal might contain:

1. A cover letter outlining the most significant points in the proposal and asking for the foundation to consider the attached proposal.

2. A cover page with the foundation's name, your school's name and the title of your proposal.

3. A table of contents listing everything within the proposal.

4. A summary of the proposal condensed to one page and including the sum of money requested, the specific purpose of the grant, the total budget of the project, and the anticipated end result.

5. The qualifications of your school's organization and staff to carry out the project.

6. A statement of the problem or need which the project is seeking to fund.

7. The goals or objectives of your project.

8. The methods which you will employ to attain your objectives and who in your organization will be accountable to see that the steps are carried out.

9. The evaluation criteria by which your program's effect will be measured.

10. Your budget in detail.

11. An appendix including evidence of your tax-exempt status, supporting documents, your latest audit, references, current operating budget, most recent IRS Form 990, names and addresses of your Board, etc.

Make sure that your final document has page numbers which correspond with your Table of Contents and that it has been thoroughly proofread by a few individuals to check for mistakes in English usage, grammar, and spelling. Make sure that the proposal is to the point and readable.

If you have no prescribed guidelines, you can write a letter proposal which is less than two pages, double spaced. A full proposal should be no more than five pages, double spaced. In any case the foundation should be contacted in advance of the proposal. The involvement of your Board can be crucial in some cases.

One support group that offers programs and services to help schools and institutions increase private financial support is CASE, *Council for Advancement and Support of Education.* They offer regional workshops on proposal writing that are highly recommended.

CASE
Suite 400, 11 Dupont Circle
Washington, DC 20036
Tel. *202/328-5900*

CASE holds many different workshops which may be beneficial to your school. In the summer they offer five-day, intensive institutes in educational fundraising as well as a variety of other topics. Also, CASE has many publications (books, monographs, and microfiche). Membership in CASE is open only to non-profit educational institutions. There is a yearly fee for membership.

One of the best pathways to a successful grant application is to know someone connected with a foundation who may be supportive. Often one finds within the school's parent body individuals who have influence or are related to someone who has; they might be willing to speak on behalf of your school.

You may have within your parent body individuals who work for a company that is willing to give **matching grants** for any donation an employee makes to a nonprofit organization. This can be an added incentive for large gifts.

Do not overlook your **State Attorney General's office.** They may have jurisdiction over bequests and legacies for which your school might qualify.

FOUNDATIONS SPECIFICALLY FORMED TO HELP WALDORF SCHOOLS

The Waldorf Educational Foundation
(Glenmede Trust Company)
This foundation was established in 1951 for the purpose of strengthening the philosophies of Rudolf Steiner as taught in North America through Waldorf education. Grants are awarded once per year, usually in the month of December. All proposals must be received no later than October 15. Grants are made to AWSNA full member schools and institutes and other pedagogical institutions affiliated with and recognized by the Association of Waldorf Schools of North America. Copies of all grant proposals must be sent to the Chairperson of AWSNA. Specific guidelines can be received by writing to:

AWSNA
3911 Bannister Rd.
Fair Oaks, CA 95628

Shared Gifting Group of the Mid-States
The Shared Gifting Group (SGG) of the Mid-States was created by Elise Ott Casper to support the work of initiatives inspired by the ideas of Rudolf Steiner and located predominantly in the central states of the U.S.A. During her lifetime, she administered the activities of the Group and provided the majority of the funds that were distributed each year. Upon her death, she bequeathed the bulk of her estate to the Rudolf

Steiner Foundation, with the recommendation that yearly distributions and grants be made from these funds with the advice of the SGG. In keeping with her wishes, the RSF established the SGG Advised Fund to which the Shared Gifting Group acts as an advisory committee.

The intentions of the Shared Gifting Group of the Mid-States are:

• To make contributions to humanity and society based on the spiritual-scientific discoveries of Rudolf Steiner.
• To direct funds toward projects that enhance community and human development and that work for the benefit of humanity and the world.
• To bring the qualities of money—purchase, loan, and gift— to consciousness, with emphasis on gift money.
• To discover and develop new ways in which donations may be made.
• To assist individuals, groups and organizations in developing ways of sharing useful information, experiences and insights that foster community and the recognition of our common bonds.

Grant application deadline is August 1. Guidelines are available upon request.

The Shared Gifting Group of the Mid-States
Rudolf Steiner Foundation
BLDG 1002 B, Thoreau Ctr., Presidio
PO Box 29915
San Francisco, CA 94129-0915
415-561-3900

Waldorf Schools Fund, Inc.

Incorporated in 1948 and registered in the state of New York, the Board meets twice yearly. This perpetual trust is limited to the benefit of schools in the United States which are full members of the Association of Waldorf Schools of North America, although the trustees have established a small fund not limited to the U.S. Write for details. All grant requests should reach the Fund Chairman prior to April 1 and September 15. Grant requests should contain:

• A brief, official letter outlining the nature of the request, supporting documents, including an institutional budget.

• Budget of the grant-application-related project. If the project is a large one, you should state how it will be completed.

• Twelve sets of the above should be sent to:

The Chairman
Waldorf Schools Fund, Inc.
1124 Rt. 21
Ghent, NY 12075

Rudolf Steiner Foundation

The Rudolf Steiner Foundation is a public not-for-profit financial service organization that supports and seeks funds from projects, organizations, and individuals whose work continues to develop Rudolf Steiner's ideas and world view. One of the basic premises of the Foundation is the recognition that the movement of money follows the spiritual intentions of human beings. Through the Foundation's Loan Funds, Gifts and Grant Funds, and Advisory Services, the Foundation mediates between those with financial capacity and those with financial need toward the common goal of renewal in society.

Founded in 1936 to serve the Anthroposophical Society in America, it was reconstituted in 1984 with its present objectives. The Foundation works with individuals who request assistance in making their charitable gifts more effective through the establishment of funds of the Foundation. Also in keeping with its charitable mission, the Foundation serves as a mediator between lenders and borrowers out of the social impulse of financial relationships.

Rudolf Steiner Foundation
BLDG 1002 B, Thoreau Ctr., Presidio
PO Box 29915
San Francisco, CA 94129-0915
415-561-3900

Chapter 12

Building for the Future of your School:
The Planned Giving Program

by

Dana Myers

A school's planned giving program is built upon the foundation established by an effective annual giving program. As a school matures, an ever widening circle of friends surrounds the school. Individuals who have made a significant personal investment in the school of their time, talents and money while their children or grandchildren are enrolled may become aware of their possible role in the school's long range plans. With a planned giving program in place, friends are often able to make far larger gifts through various techniques of financial planning, estate planning and tax planning than they have been able to make with an outright gift of cash.

Unlike an Annual Giving Program, which supports the operational expenses of a school, planned gifts are often used to fund a school's long term goals, such as funding of an endowment or support for capital needs, land acquisition or building campaigns. The reason for this is that many of the techniques employed in a planned giving program do not provide immediate income to the school.

When should a school initiate a planned giving program? Once a school's annual giving program is solidly established, the trustees and staff should begin to explore their readiness for a planned giving program. To have a successful planned giving program, a school must be about to communicate a clear vision of its future, to communicate why a bequest or other gift is needed to secure that future. There must be stability and leadership from the Board and staff, committed to champion the cause of the program for a minimum of 5 to 10 years. The school must be in a strong financial position so that donors can be confident that their gifts will be well-managed, and that restricted or endowment funds will be maintained with integrity. It should be understood by the Board and College of Teachers that a planned giving program is a long-term investment to secure the future of the school. It is often 20+ years before a program begins to bring in funds to the school; yet a planned giving program requires an on-going investment of staff and volunteer resources.

The success of a planned giving program depends upon a school's ability to clearly communicate its mission and goals, and its ability to build and maintain relationships with its supporters. As in any relationship, the journey to discover common goals and values between a school and its donors can be a fulfilling and enriching one. One of the benefits of a planned giving program is that many of the mechanisms used for making a "planned gift" often help a school develop long term relationships with its donors.

Just as it is the teachers' role to help students discover their capacities which they will use throughout their lives, a planned giving program, properly administered, can help a school's supporters discover their capacities for making significant financial gifts that will help carry the school into the future.

There is no "model" planned giving program for a Waldorf school. The size and structure of the program should be determined by the staff and Board resources that are available to promote, administer and manage the program successfully. Though staff do not need to be tax lawyers or estate planners to initiate a Planned Giving Program, both the development staff and the trustees need to have a basic knowledge of the methods or "vehicles" available to donors for making their gifts. It is important that the Board of Trustees have a clear understanding of their role and responsibilities for a planned giving program, that staff have the necessary training and resources to serve the needs of prospective donors.

The role of the development office can vary depending upon the expertise of the staff and the needs of the donor. What estate planning services a school can provide are often quite limited; therefore, it is important to have available people who can be used as resources when a program is established. A school should have legal counsel who are knowledgeable in charitable estate planning. They may wish to draw upon this counsel's expertise in both setting up the program and in meetings with prospective donors and their financial advisors.

Some prospective donors will approach the school with a gift plan already developed by their financial advisors; other donors may know that they would like to make a gift to the school but wish the school to help them plan what gift would be best for helping to meet the school's future needs as well as their personal financial goals.

"... solicitation, planning and administration of a charitable gift is a complex process involving philanthropic, personal, financial, and tax considerations, and often involves professionals from various disciplines whose goals should include working together to structure a gift that achieves a fair and proper balance between the interests of the donor and the purposes of the charitable institution."
– excerpt from "Model Standards of Practice for the Charitable Gift Planner," National Committee on Planned Giving and the American Council on Gift Annuities, May 7, 1991.

A planned giving program is an important part of the development work of any mature school that has clearly determined its long range goals. With compelling goals for a school's future, and a staff and Board who are dedicated to reaching those goals, a planned giving program can make a significant contribution to the health of a school. It is an aspect of fundraising that is technical, complex and ever-changing, but is an aspect which is most rewarding and worthwhile.

Resources:
The National Committee on Planned Giving
233 McCrea Street, Suite 400
Indianapolis, IN 46225
http://www.ncpg.org

The National Society of Fund Raising Executives
1101 King Street, Suite 700
Alexandria, VA 22314-2967
http://www.nsfre.org

The Rudolf Steiner Foundation
P.O. Box 29915
San Francisco, CA 94129-0915
mail@RSFoundation.org

Many community foundations provide assistance to non-profits in the area of planned giving.

Chapter 13

The Budget and Internal Controls

by

Dave Alsop and Agaf Dancy

One of the key elements to the success of any organization is the ability to manage money. Every Waldorf school is faced with the challenge of managing its available resources, of creating new resources, and of meeting its obligations to the community. Typically, the tool used to meet this challenge on an annual basis is the school budget.

It must be said at the outset that Waldorf Schools have a special task to fulfill with respect to their financial aspects, and that this task should penetrate and be visible both in the budgeting process and in the budget itself. This task is to do everything possible to foster and encourage true brotherhood in the school community. We do not want our Waldorf schools to become places where education is perceived as a commodity to be bought and sold, where the teachers are seen simply as employees paid for their work, and where appeals for funds are perceived as a sign of weakness. We do want to establish and make visible the fact that the school must be a community of dedicated teachers and parents, with specific tasks incumbent upon each. This is very difficult in today's consumer oriented society, and yet steps must be made. The budget process gives us very real opportunities in this direction, as we shall see.

A budget can be defined as a document that translates the plans of the school, to be accomplished during a specific period of time, into financial terms. It clearly delineates the scope of activity for the year, as determined by the faculty, the Board of Trustees, and the parents of the school. It also must provide continuity between the past years and the future years, especially in terms of capital income and expenses and long term debt. The budget is not a straightjacket or a metal box that confines the activity of the school. It is rather the framework within which to meet the objectives of the year.

Budgets take many forms in our schools, varying from a single page summary to documents dozens of pages in length. All budgets consist of informed estimates of income and expenses. There are actually two budgets that should be prepared each year—a capital budget and an operating budget. The capital budget should address all of those non-consumable items that will last into the future. The operating budget accounts for short-term activity, for the items that are used up, salaries and payment for services received during the specific year. Each of these budgets will be taken up in the sections that follow.

The Operating Budget

It is imperative that the income be at least equal to the expenses in the annual operating budget. It is becoming commonplace for many non-profit organizations to budget for a surplus on a yearly basis, in order to establish cash reserves as a kind of contingency fund. There is no problem whatsoever when a non-profit organization shows a profit (surplus) at the end of the year. However, a school is in very real trouble when the budget shows a deficit—expense higher than income—for any length of time. The inability to meet financial obligations to one's creditors as well as internally to faculty and staff will soon result in the loss of confidence in the school. The school's ability to operate is based almost entirely upon the ability to inspire confidence and to keep it, not only in the classroom but also in the business office. Therefore, it is essential that as Waldorf schools we strive for a balanced operating budget with a modest profit, if possible.

As stated above, the operating budget is the document that presents the plan for operating income and expenses, within a specific time period (also called "the fiscal year"). It is focused on purchases and costs that have a limited life—usually one year or less—and on income sources that are usually contractual and also time limited. What follows is a listing of summary income and expense categories that are typical for Waldorf schools. This list corresponds to the categories requested in the annual AWSNA Financial Survey. Typically, such categories are called "accounts." Together with asset and liability accounts (discussed later) they comprise the entire "chart of accounts," also sometimes referred to as the General Ledger. Each account may have multiple sub-accounts that appear on a more detailed presentation of the budget for the Finance

Committee to scrutinize. At the Board level and for presentation to parents and the public (such as in an Annual Report), the summary level shown here is sufficient.

Your school's bookkeeper and/or accountant may find this list helpful in setting up your school's accounting system. Ideally, this will be done on a computer to facilitate budget manipulation and financial tracking. Please refer to the chapter on "Technology and Administration" for further discussion of computers and accounting software.

Operating Budget Income and Expense Accounts

Income:
Tuition and fees*
Other programs (after care, summer camp, etc.)
Investment/interest
Fundraising activity (Bazaar, etc.)
Contributions/grants
Misc. income
Total income:

Expenses:
Instructional:
       Faculty salaries
       Benefits/payroll taxes
       Faculty tuition remission*
       Financial aid (non-faculty)*
       Professional development
       Supplies and misc. expenses
Other programs (after-care, summer camp, and etc.):
       Salaries
       Benefits/payroll taxes
       Supplies and misc. expenses
Plant Operation and Maintenance:
       Salaries
       Benefits/payroll taxes
       Repairs, maintenance, utilities
       Building rental/mortgage expense
       Supplies and misc. expenses
General, administrative and fundraising:
       Salaries

Benefits/payroll taxes
Publications, advertising, events
Depreciation
Supplies and misc. expenses
Total Expense

Increase in Net Assets (income less expense)

* Note that in this suggested format, tuition and fees are for all students, including faculty children and those on tuition assistance at full value. This is in order to make visible to ourselves the expense associated with faculty tuition remission and financial aid (which appears under instructional expenses).

The detail to which a school goes depends upon its own needs and style of management and the complexity of the school's operations. The school may choose, for instance, to identify certain "classes" of income and expense in order to facilitate the creation of the budget and tracking actual income and expense against it through the year. These classes are sometimes called "cost centers" or "divisions" in for-profit businesses and represent recognizably distinct areas of program or activity. For instance, for budgeting purposes one might identify the preschool-kindergarten, grades and high school as distinct classes. They might then be presented in separate columns to the right of the income and expense accounts with a total column at the far right. Alternatively, they might be presented on separate pages, using all the same income and expense accounts, with a total page summarizing them all. An important point to note here is that this method of presentation, while very useful for building up the budget from its basic components, should not lead us into a fragmentary consciousness with kindergarten teachers pitted against grades or high school teachers over who contributes most or costs most. The school is an organic whole.

What is the process for creating the operating budget? First, the budget period or fiscal year must be established. Usually schools begin and end the fiscal year in the summer, as that is a more natural rhythm in terms of the financial activity in a school than the calendar year would be. New tuition payments begin in the advent of the new school year. By linking the fiscal year and the school year, it is easy to compare the budget projections with the actual fiscal experience. The government will recognize any fiscal year for reporting purposes.

Next, the school community must be able to articulate plans and priorities for the year. This involves asking such questions as: Do we need a salary increase, and what will it cost? Should we have Spanish as well as German next year, and what will it cost? What is the likely increase in our health insurance next year, and should we try to offer a dental plan to the faculty and staff? One soon realizes that the budget process is a product of the planning process, and that a clear vision of the long-term goals of the school is helpful in the yearly budgeting process. One can picture that each year another step is taken toward that long-term vision, and that the budget is there to identify that step and to support it. Generally, the faculty assumes primary responsibility for establishing the plans and priorities for the coming year as they relate to the pedagogy. Administrative staff and the Board may identify other needs that should be considered. In general, any individual or group that has primary responsibility for an aspect of the budget should be invited to offer input into the process at this point, perhaps by means of a survey of needs and goals for the coming year. Many schools have "planning committees" which work on these questions and make suggestions to the Faculty and Board about plans and priorities.

This is one of the areas where schools have the opportunity to weld their communities together. The inclusion of parents and community members in discussions about future growth and expansion of the school's activities is a necessary step in the healthy development of a Waldorf school. They will be the primary source of financial support for the school, and if we are to foster an atmosphere of brotherhood and financial responsibility that goes beyond simply paying one's tuition when due, then meaningful inclusion in the development of the plan is required. This is not to suggest that by virtue of financial support alone one is to be included, but rather that the inclusion may awaken understanding of the true circumstances of the school community.

Once the program requirements are identified, estimates of costs must be made. This is where historical information is very helpful. It is necessary to keep accurate records of past experience, because a good deal of guesswork can be eliminated by referring to past budgets, financial compilations and statements, and notes made as one goes along regarding cost increases. This is typically undertaken by the administrative staff (and this is where having the school's financial records computerized can be so helpful). In this way a preliminary expense budget is developed which shows the estimated cost of the new program. Concurrent with this, each teacher and staff member should be interviewed, to establish the more detailed needs of their specific subject areas and classes. The result of this process is that the expense side of the preliminary operating budget is compiled.

The next step is to estimate the income side of the budget. This requires an evaluation of enrollment and of tuition levels, as the majority of the income will be from tuition. Regardless of the method used for determining fees and collecting tuition, a realistic estimate is crucial. It is a good plan to be somewhat conservative in estimating the enrollment, rather than place the school at risk by overestimation. Every class teacher needs to speak about the size of his class, and to his sense of the stability of his enrollment. This is done in the Faculty meetings, and the data is compiled and passed on to the Board. Each family is asked about its intentions for the next year, to try to get a feeling for the stability of the situation. A strategy used by many schools is to establish a deadline for protected re-enrollment (which works well if there are waiting lists) and/or for an "early enrollment discount" to get the numbers firmed up as early as possible. Along with tuition income, there may be other fees that need to be evaluated, such as day care or school bus fees. The administrative staff should do a careful analysis of the potential income from these sources and refer them to the Board.

The other primary source of income for the operating budget is donations to operations. Most schools have fund raising programs designed to provide non-fee income. Appeals, auctions, fairs, and other special events are common. The most common rationale for these programs is that they help to keep the tuition costs as low as possible, and that they promote community spirit. As with all sources of income, however, they should be thoroughly researched and based upon a track record when budgeted. There is the danger of budgeting an unrealistic hope, especially if an idea has no history. An event that does not pan out can cause as much damage to the budget as the unexpected withdrawal of a number of students. Once events and fundraising have been established, they are indeed a necessary support to the operating budget.

Working with the income side of the budget will of necessity require the consideration of the expense side. This is why one should begin by identifying the desired program, so that a "target" is established for the income side. The first attempt should be to determine what it would take to meet the whole program. This may prove to be vastly expensive, requiring tuition increases of intolerable proportions, or it may not. The key point is that even if the program cannot be funded in its entirety and must be cut back, useful information has been gathered about goals and priorities that can be shared with the community. It is very important that the parent body know that "The 5% tuition increase made possible a 5% salary increase, and that rather than increase tuition 10%, the Board has decided to postpone the retirement fund." This kind of information can inspire members of the community to the most remarkable action, even if it sometimes takes a long time. The Board must share its hesitations and fears, as well as its successes, to allow community awakening and involvement.

A good strategy in presenting the priorities identified in the budgeting process is to establish a baseline budget that includes everything you can of your goals while holding to a balanced budget. Remaining goals can then be listed in priority sequence, showing which will be funded first as additional money becomes available. This is preferable to a budget which overreaches itself and must then have items cut.

Prior to adoption, the proposed operating budget should be made available to interested parents and community members for their input. All parents should be apprised of the assumptions regarding tuition and program changes, and their input should be considered. If this is to be meaningful input, it should be solicited early enough in the process that it could in fact have an influence on the outcome. There should be real choices on the table. Otherwise, it could easily be viewed as a sham intended to justify decisions that have in fact already been made elsewhere. The result could be apathy, loss of confidence and low turnout. It should be made clear to everyone from the outset, however, that while the broader community's input is genuinely desired, the Board of Trustees is the body that will be responsible for the final adoption of the budget.

This process takes time to complete, and it is very important that adequate time be given to ensure that all parties are fully included. It is not desirable to rush through important decisions and discussions. Most schools begin the budget process in earnest in November, with a target completion date in February or March. This gives the community time to be involved, and allows tuition levels to be set prior to the re-enrollment process, which must begin in the spring.

Generally, the Board will review and revise the proposed budget towards the end of the school year, when enrollment for the new school year is more certain. At that time, if projections were made realistically in the first place, only minor adjustments should be necessary. If some cutbacks are required or if additional goals can be funded, this should be done by the Board based on the priorities agreed upon in the earlier process if at all possible. May or June is not the ideal time of year to ask people to participate in meetings to decide budget issues.

Monitoring and Reporting Performance

The Board (or its Finance Committee, if the Board meets less frequently) should receive monthly statements (reports) from the Business Manager or Treasurer accounting for actual income and expenditures in comparison to the budget, and pointing out any difficulties which may arise. The budget is a guideline rather than a fixed document, and the Board may make exceptions to its provisions, as necessary. Aside from exceptions agreed to by the Board, however, all responsible parties should be held accountable for keeping within the limits established in the budget. These monthly reports should include a Balance Sheet, a Report of Income and Expenses, and a Cash Flow Report. Both the Income and Expense Report and the Cash Flow Report should provide a budget to actual comparison for the period just ended, both monthly and cumulative.

A Balance Sheet is a listing of all the school's assets and liabilities. Assets include cash in checking and savings accounts, money owed by parents (accounts receivable) and buildings, furniture and equipment owned. Liabilities include money owed for current purchases (accounts payable), taxes withheld from earnings and owed to the government, mortgage balances and other debt. The difference between Assets and Liabilities, or Net Assets, is the sum of what the school would be "worth" if everything were sold off and all accounts were settled. This is the figure that grows or shrinks from year to year as the school has a surplus or ends the year with a loss. A sample of Balance Sheet accounts follows. As with the Income and Expense accounts presented earlier, these are taken from the AWSNA Annual Survey and represent a summary of the accounts most commonly in use by the schools:

Balance Sheet

Assets:
Cash and short-term investments
Accounts Receivable
        Standard receivables
        Contributions receivable
Scholarship Fund

118

Building Fund
Endowment Fund
Other current assets
Land and Building (if owned)*
Furniture, equipment and other*
Total Assets:

Liabilities and Net Assets:
Accounts payable
Tax withheld
Other current liabilities**
Mortgage
Other long term debt
Total Liabilities:

Net Assets:
Unrestricted
Temporarily restricted
Permanently restricted
Total Net Assets:

Liabilities plus Net Assets:
(should equal Total Assets)

*Net of depreciation
**Include deferred revenues

Note that recently adopted reporting standards for non-profits call for the listing of Net Assets in three categories. Unrestricted funds are those over which the Board has full discretionary authority (including funds that the Board has "designated" or set aside for a specific purpose). Temporarily restricted funds consist of gift money received for a purpose designated by the donor and not yet spent for that purpose (formerly carried as a Fund under Liabilities). Permanently restricted funds consist of gift money received for a purpose designated by the donor that may not be spent (typically, an endowment whose interest may be used but whose principal may not be touched). Your financial officer or accountant will typically prepare statements showing movement of funds into and out of all three fund categories as part of your overall Income and Expense Reports. For the present, we are concerned with the Operating Budget, which is reflected in the Income and Expense Report for Unrestricted funds.

The Income and Expense Report tells the Board how well you are doing in relation to the overall budget. It typically shows columns for Actual, Budget and Variance (difference between them, expressed as dollars or as a percent of budget), with income and expense accounts listed on the left as they were shown on your budget. This can be for the current month only or for the fiscal year to date (both reports should be prepared monthly). It is important to project the yearly budget into 12 monthly components, as many items occur at a specific, predictable moment in time (e.g., insurance payments or one-time fundraisers) as opposed to those that happen a bit each month. You must plan for both kinds of items in order to make an educated estimate of the correct anticipated income and expenses as of a given month. This projection will allow the comparison of actual to anticipated income and expense on a monthly basis, and it will soon become clear if the overall budget is correct. It is critical to the financial health of the school that the budget be closely monitored, as well as the cash.

A Cash Flow Report shows the actual cash which has entered the checking, savings and short-term investment accounts and that which has been spent in each month, and compares that figure with the anticipated activity. It combines aspects of the Balance Sheet with the Income and Expense Statement in order to show the flow of "liquid" assets. This is the report that makes it possible to see if and when the school is going to run out of cash, irrespective of how much net income the Income and Expense Report is showing. Why are these different? Because included in the Income are the tuition amounts you have billed, regardless of whether they have been collected; likewise, purchases you have made but not yet paid for are listed as expenses. This is in accordance with the "accrual method" of accounting, which is what your school should be using (as will be discussed later). The Cash Flow Report (and the cash flow budget) eliminates any income or expense activity that doesn't result in a change to your bank balances: such items as invoicing families and expensing depreciation. It also adds in transactions that don't show up on an Income and Expense report but do change your bank balance: payment of mortgage principal or outstanding loans or the purchase of equipment. It thus shows the "fat" and "lean" months in the school's financial activity with respect to cash on hand and allows for firmer control of the timing of large purchases. This report should document actual funds available through the year.

Unexpected events do happen—3 children may withdraw; the liability insurance premium may double in mid-year; the school bus could break down; parents may fail to pay tuition on time—and the financial picture of the school is affected. Through proper reporting, these events can be taken into account and the necessary steps taken so that the school does not unexpectedly find itself in a cash-poor situation. The effective use of these reports will result in good cash management, and good budget management, and they will give confidence in the way the finances of the school are being handled to a broad range of Board members, faculty members and parents.

There are several areas that need to be very closely monitored and which provide early warnings of difficulties. Tuition income is always the largest income producer for the budget and needs the closest scrutiny. It is imperative that large receivables are not allowed to accumulate, that is, that tuition is paid on time! Many schools have adopted policies that prohibit students from attending school if the tuition bill becomes seriously past due (usually 90+ days) in an effort to reduce the possibility of the tuition going unpaid. The school will be in serious difficulty if the Board is uninformed of growing tuition balances and/or fails to take action to collect the tuition. The point is that the school needs clear-cut policies for collection of tuition that spell out what will be done, and when, if families fall behind in their payments. Many schools now also require families paying on an installment basis to use a tuition management company that handles billing and collection. Many also require families to take out tuition insurance (optional for those paying in full).

Fundraising and donations should also be monitored very closely. It is all too easy to balance the budget by increasing the expected income from fundraising, but is that truly realistic? The fundraising plan should be able to articulate the months when the income will be received, and then this should be validated through experience. This also gives the Board plenty of time to consider its options should a given event fail to perform as expected.

Accounting Procedures and Administrative Efficiency
Who should manage your school's finances and be responsible for guiding the budget process? Perhaps the willing and well-intentioned nurse on your school's Board is not the best choice. Your school's future is literally in the hands of the people who carry this responsibility. Entrust it to individuals who have the requisite experience and skills and don't

expect them to manage it in their spare time, as volunteers or on top of already full work loads. These people can then be surrounded and supported by others from the community, parent body and faculty who will form a Finance Committee, reporting to the Board.

Working as a team will help to ensure the accuracy of reporting and minimize the possibility of error. In order to further reduce the possibility of error—or embezzlement—certain basic internal controls should be established. None of us likes to think that unsavory things can happen in our Waldorf schools, but they can and have. Schools have been placed in jeopardy of closing in the past because of grievous errors or misconduct. Among the most basic protections the school can put in place is to provide for a separation of functions and for oversight of financial transactions by disinterested parties. The treasurer should regularly review the work of the business manager and/or bookkeeper. Many schools also engage the services of an outside accounting firm to review the accounts and prepare reports each month. The person who prepares the checks should not be the one authorized to sign them. Checks for large sums may require two signatures. While most transactions at the school are by check, the occasional payment by cash or use of petty cash should be recorded using appropriate receipt books, signed or initialed by the person receiving the cash. These receipts should then be reconciled to deposit records. Checking and other account balances should must be reconciled on a monthly basis, as soon as bank statements have arrived, and monthly reports must be prepared for the Treasurer and Finance Committee.

The school's accounting records should be maintained on the accrual rather than the cash basis of accounting. Inherent in this method is the recording of tuition and other revenues when billed and the recognition of expenses when incurred. As the timing of the payment or receipt of cash can differ significantly from the timing of the underlying transactions, the accrual basis will be more accurate and provide a better foundation for making financial and operating decisions. In particular, the effectiveness of budgetary controls will be enhanced. In the accrual method one uses an Accounts Receivable account to record bills sent to parents but not yet collected, and an Accounts Payable account to track purchases made and bills received that have not yet been paid by the school. Some financial officers also favor tracking the difference between tuition collected and tuition "earned" (through months taught) as another step in assuring that the "snapshot" taken of the school's accounts at month-end is as accurate as possible. That seems a bit excessive to us, however, unless the school is in danger of closing mid-year, in which case the unearned portion of tuition would indeed need to be refunded! If the school's fiscal year is set so that it follows the school year there should be little or no carry-over of unearned income from one year to the next.

Many of the traditional chores of month-end reconciliation and report creation have been eliminated or greatly simplified by the widespread use of computerized accounting software. If your school is still managing its accounts by hand, it's time to change! Please refer to the chapter on Technology for Administration. Programs like Quickbooks have automated and integrated many accounting activities. You will never post to a General Ledger, or run a Trial Balance, again!

Given the school's fiduciary responsibilities in holding restricted contributions, it is important that the restricted accounts be properly maintained. Specifically, close attention should be given to receipting and dispersing Temporarily Restricted funds such that a clear accounting can be given of all disbursements made for the restricted purposes. While it is not strictly necessary, some schools find it easiest to physically segregate such funds in separate checking or savings accounts.

The school should consider utilizing a purchase order system to assist in the control over large purchases. A reasonable limit should be placed on purchases not requiring a formal purchase order. At the same time, controls should not be so rigid as to seriously impair the normal conduct of business. Teachers and others often need to make purchases of consumable supplies and should not be required to get prior approval for every purchase. A reasonable approach is to establish a discretionary budget for each class teacher and special subject teacher for a portion of the supplies that will be used each year. Teachers may then submit receipts for reimbursement up to the limit of their discretionary budgets without needing prior approval. It should not be difficult to prepare a monthly accounting for them of their usage and remaining balance.

The Capital Budget

The capital budget is the budget that accounts for the long-term assets of the school. Each year, purchases are made which will not have to be made again the following year because the items will still be useable. These items will become a part of the overall net worth of the school, subject to depreciation. Buildings, equipment, farm implements, science equipment, furniture, and so on, are examples of capital items.

Capital items are of such a nature that they should not be thought of as paid for by operating income in any one year, but rather as something acquired for the future that transcends the fixed limits of the operating budget. Yet real cash must be spent for these items and the plans to use this cash must be reflected in the Cash Flow Budget discussed previously.

Where do the funds come from to pay for these (often) big-ticket items whose useful life will continue beyond the end of the fiscal year? It's not right to expense these items, and try to pay for them, exclusively out of the operating budget. Even if it could, what the parents pay in tuition for the current year should not have to shoulder the full cost of a new building that will last thirty years. It is appropriate for the operating budget to contribute a reasonable sum to cover costs associated with using and maintaining the physical plant. Repairs and maintenance are a routine part of the operating budget. By expensing depreciation in the operating budget, a fair share of the costs associated with future major repairs (of the roof, for instance) or replacement (of obsolete equipment) can be charged to the operating budget in addition to the expenses for routine maintenance. It's not good enough, though, to simply "book" the depreciation expense. A corresponding transfer needs to be made to the plant fund, so that the cash will be there when it's needed. Moreover, for this to be a transfer of more than empty promises, the operating budget must not chronically rack up deficits. There must be actual cash accumulating in the bank that will be there when it's needed.

How will the buildings and major equipment be purchased in the first place, if not within the operating budget? Through a development program, and through grants and gift money. This is quite different from the fundraising done to support the operating budget. A development program is undertaken to ensure that the school has the resources necessary to operate in the future, not in the present. By securing long-term commitments from community members to support the school building programs, or library growth, or furniture and equipment needs, the development program is ensuring that the school will remain sound for children who are not currently enrolled. It is also proper that gift money be used to make a lasting impact upon the educational experience, through the purchase of capital items. We must strive to educate our school communities to the fact that the physical body of the school—the buildings, playgrounds, furniture and equipment—should be funded out of a desire to see the school healthy and strong for future generations of teachers and children. Our current tuition makes only a modest contribution toward that goal.

Annual Reporting and the Annual Report

As a conclusion to the budget process, each school should distribute an Annual Report to its community and friends. There needs to be a closure to the financial year, and a statement of how well the goals were met during the past year will provide that. An instrument designed to recognize the success and to acknowledge the shortfalls of the financial life of the school will go a long way towards strengthening the school community. Acknowledgment of and thanks to the sources of help—from individuals or from foundations or from other organizations—would help each community to see that it is not isolated and without friends. The sharing of the unattained goals need not be an admission of failure, but rather can become the opportunity for someone previously uninvolved to join in and help.

There are other reports that must be prepared on an annual basis as well, of a more prosaic nature. The Year-End Financial Statements form the basis for the information that will go into the Annual Report and (for U. S. schools) the required IRS Form 990 for non-profit organizations. The school would do well to engage the services of an accounting firm to help tie together the loose ends, record depreciation and sale or disposal of assets properly, and so on as part of the process of preparing these year-end reports. Payroll and tax reports must also be filed, though generally on a quarterly and calendar year basis. Again, as with the year-end closing and reports, it would be good to consider using an accounting firm or a firm specializing in payroll to help manage the specialized reporting required. Likewise, if the school provides a pension plan such as TIAA/CREF, it will be required to file Form 5500 C/R following the end of the plan year. Your pension company should provide you with the information and instructions you need to do this. Lastly, remember to file the annual Corporate Report and fee for your state! Don't jeopardize your corporate status by forgetting to file.

Conclusion

A Waldorf school's budget is not in itself that different from the budget of other non-profit organizations. There is a certain amount of income on the one hand and a certain number of expenses on the other hand, and they are either of a capital or an operating nature. Where the budget can begin to assume new dimensions is if we carry as a leading thought that we are not only trying to operate in a traditional, fiscally responsible way, but that we are also attempting to awaken a sense of social responsibility and financial brotherhood. This is not easy, and we are constantly seduced by old forms of thinking and the need for expediency.

If we are to avoid Waldorf education being perceived merely as a commodity, then the income side—particularly the way we deal with tuition and scholarships—must be much more a topic of study and exploration within our faculties and our Boards, and ultimately within our parent bodies. Likewise, to avoid our teachers becoming merely paid employees rather than individuals committed to the future of the school, we must scrutinize the expense side of the budget and penetrate what we are really doing when we create salary scales and hourly wages. Finally, if we are going to be able to appeal for funds out of a position of strength rather than weakness, we must fully understand the necessity to build a healthy physical body for the school.

Above all, the budget must be a statement of the vision and intentions of the school community. The success of that budget will be seen in how well it can reflect to the community the deeper initiative that is fundamental to the Waldorf school.

Chapter 14

Compensation:
Salaries and Benefit Administration

by

Lynn Kern

Rudolf Steiner described a threefold social order in which economic brotherhood, equality of rights and spiritual freedom were each recognized as fundamentally important. Building this new social consciousness was intended to provide hope and meaning to the world.

One manifestation of these ideas is the Waldorf school movement. Founded as a cultural institution, Waldorf schools seek to create free human beings whose personal potential is maximized and who contribute consciously and purposefully to the world as adults. It is a sign of our times that we do not think of schools as cultural institutions. Instead, we view them as economic enterprises, institutions which create a product which is purchased by parents for consumption by their children.

The truth is that our schools produce no product, but rather are themselves consumers of products. It is the capital created in the economic realm which flows into our schools through parents and other supporters which permits the sustenance of the independent cultural institution which is a Waldorf school.

Compensation in the Ideal

Understanding this difference is a key to any discussion of compensation in a Waldorf school. Waldorf teachers are expected to be creative artists in the classroom. They are asked to learn the factual material related to the subject, make it their own and then bring it forth in a unique and personal way that meets the needs of all the students in the class, allowing the students opportunities to make the material their own as well. Waldorf administrators must also bring a creative impulse to their work, developing and implementing systems and processes that allow the spirit of the school to reveal itself as a living and evolving organism.

A key to supporting and nurturing this creative impulse is a salary that meets the human needs of those doing the work. There cannot be true freedom in the cultural sphere without the economic sphere making it possible.

Compensation is the single largest cost in a Waldorf school. Compensation covers several areas, of which salary is only one aspect. Other items which must be considered in any discussion of compensation include health care, sabbaticals, a provision for retirement, and a variety of other minor benefits. As the largest line item on our budget, the way in which we think about and provide for compensation is a significant reflection of the way in which the community sees itself, and a major opportunity to shape the school for the future.

Setting salary levels appropriately in a Waldorf school requires a high level of social awareness and constant conscious work. The easy answer in today's world is that salaries must be based on the work performed, a belief that comes from a presumption that the school is buying the labor of its teachers and staff. However, the threefold social order suggests instead that the salary is provided to meet the human needs of the individual so that she can place her skills and talents into the service of the school.

Although it can be difficult, there is a creative tension that can exist between these two polar views. At the one extreme is the picture that everyone who does the same work is paid the same amount. The opposing picture says that compensation is not for work, but to meet the unique needs of the person doing the work so that the work can go forward. Accordingly, each person needs a unique compensation package that addresses her unique situation.

We can start by suggesting that salaries must make possible some reasonable standard of living. What is viewed as "fair" must strike a balance between the standard of living of the parent body and the standard of living provided to the faculty. If a salary structure or level does not "feel right" to the general community, no amount of justification or rationalization will make it right. People must feel good about salaries, both the faculty receiving the salary and the parents who provide it. It follows that a healthy compensation package requires active joint parent and faculty participation in the life of the school.

During the pioneer stages of school development, there are often inadequate resources. Teachers often make do with amazingly little, both in the classroom and in the area of their personal finances. This can work well in the beginning. However, as the school grows and matures, it is critical that the community remain conscious of the inadequate salary levels being provided and work to remedy them. If low salaries are no longer consciously recognized and become accepted, then problems can and do arise.

As consumers of financial resources, teachers feel guilty about asking for more. Budget shortfalls are often met with, "What can I give up?" and teachers rarely ask for salary increases. Meanwhile, parents feel guilty if they require teachers to work at insufficient salaries and to do without such basic human needs as medical and dental care. Creating a healthy social life requires a vital, communicating, interpenetrating community. Everyone must feel confident that the each of the others is pulling her own oar so that, working together, the ship can move forward.

It is this conscious common opinion of what is to be expected, of what is fair, that forms the basis of the rights life. During the early stages of a school's existence, this common opinion can easily be shared between the few people involved. But as the school grows and matures, these conscious perceptions need to be formalized and written down so that they can be shared by the full community.

This shared vision of what is to be expected can include the provision that different people have different needs and as a result require different compensation. However, a truly needs based salary is only socially supportable when we recognize that an individual's unique needs arise out of her karma; unless this conviction is widely and firmly held in the faculty, a needs based salary structure quickly falls by the wayside.

Practical Advice

Needs based salary structures are not easily supportable in the legal environment of the United States. As a school works to formalize its vision for the healthy administration of compensation, it must balance its desire to work out of an understanding of the threefold social order with a recognition of current employment law in the United States. Schools are urged to seek legal counsel when attempting to develop a needs based salary structure, and to make the determination as to the amount of risk of expensive litigation they are willing to undertake. Unfortunately, this is an area in which the old maxim rings most true, for it does seem that "No good deed goes unpunished."

Given the need for salary structures to reflect the living sense of what's right in a particular community and the legal constriction described above, it is difficult to prescribe a specific salary structure that can work well for many schools. In this area two offerings only can be provided, both of them under the heading of things to be avoided.

The first is in the area of adding to someone's salary if the faculty member has dependents. These dependent allowances, especially when tied to a colleague's status as the head of household, are to be avoided. While this addition is an attempt to recognize the real added expenses that a colleague with a family may have, marital status and the existence of children are prohibited questions when considering a candidate for employment and are presumed on their face to be evidence of illegal discrimination. This same logic is generally applied to compensation cases, and the school's salary structure will be struck down. While it is possible to make a case that, according to a very narrow interpretation of the law, a plan of this sort may be legal, generally speaking Waldorf schools cannot afford to make this argument.

The second practice to be avoided is creating a lower salary structure for special subject teachers than for class teachers. All colleagues who have made the conscious choice to place their talents at the service of the school on a full time basis should be compensated in a similar fashion. The responsibility that class teachers undertake for the relationship between the school and families is matched by different responsibilities that special subject teachers carry for the school and is not an appropriate basis for salary differentiation. This same caveat applies to kindergarten and nursery teachers, who are not part time teachers, but rather class teachers who have all their teaching periods compressed into a morning schedule.

Recognizing the difficulty of implementing a true needs based salary structure, schools have fallen back on more traditional methods of setting salaries. Criteria which are often used include:

• Years of teaching/administrative experience in a Waldorf school. Some schools recognize only the years spent at their own institution; others recognize years of experience at any Waldorf school.

• Years of teaching/administrative experience elsewhere. This type of experience is often capped so that an experienced teacher who has not spent any time in a Waldorf school is not compensated at the same level as a teacher who has spent her entire career teaching out of Waldorf pedagogy.

• Completion of a Waldorf teacher or administrative training program. One interesting variation used in some schools is a training increment that is paid for those who have successfully completed the training; those who have not yet completed the training will have their training expenses paid by the school, up to the amount of the training increment, each year until the training is completed.

• Possession of advanced degrees.

Which of these criteria are used, and what dollar amounts are attached to each of them, must be worked through in each community. It is recommended that a school form a salary work group which has the ongoing responsibility of dealing with salary structure creation and adjustment. Membership on the group should include faculty members, Board members, parents and representatives from the school's administration. In this way it is possible to ensure that the structure that is created is economically viable in both the short and long term and that the plan will represent a shared picture of what is fair for both faculty and the parent body.

Benefit Administration

Once a school has done the difficult work of establishing a salary structure that reflects the will and vision of the community, it must address the issue of related benefits. These benefits include tuition remission, medical and dental care, retirement, sabbaticals and professional training and development. Again, these issues must be brought into balance with each other and must work within the overall funding that is available for personnel needs.

For example, when a school is new and salaries are relatively low, it will be important that the school provide medical and dental care for its faculty and for their families. This is an area in which individuals on a low salary may feel forced to scrimp, even when they recognize the risks that come from deferring needed medical attention. A school must see that its faculty is provided with coverage, so that it can ensure the faculty's continued ability to provide for the needs of the children.

Another benefit that is provided when salaries are low is tuition remission. This allows the children of faculty members to attend the Waldorf school, rather than creating the uncomfortable position of finding Waldorf teachers who are unable to offer their own children the benefits of the Waldorf education they are providing to the children of others.

As the school grows and develops, the size of this tuition remission benefit can become quite large. A school should give consideration as to whether remission will be given in all cases, or whether faculty members should apply for tuition reduction through the assistance program as do all other low income parents. In some communities this may create a better sense of "fairness" between the parent body and the faculty, even though the results may be the same. Another perspective is that teachers are already greatly subsidizing the education through time away from family, effort beyond what teachers in other schools are asked to give, and unusually low salaries. The greater community should support the teacher's children, so that they are allowed to attend the Waldorf school .

Some schools limit the amount of tuition aid given, perhaps to 40 or 50% of the tuition for the child. If this is the case, then some adjustment would be necessary to either the tuition assistance process or the tuition remission policy to create the intended result. For example, in a school which limits tuition assistance to 40%, remission of 60% may be offered to full time faculty. Then those faculty members with low family income may apply for tuition assistance, and may receive the equivalent of full remission.

Those schools where there is a wide salary spread between new teachers and the most experienced generally avoid this tuition assistance approach to the remission benefit. They recognize correctly that salaries and benefits are those things which enable one to place their talents at the service of the organization. Generally, younger faculty members need the benefit of remission; more experienced (older) faculty are less interested in remission and need the higher salary to help provide for their approaching retirement. Again, it is clear that one cannot be prescriptive in this area; schools must work actively through a proper understanding of the threefold social order with all members of the community to develop a salary and benefit package that is "right" for the given school.

Funding for training and professional development should also be supported by the school, so that each individual is encouraged and supported in her quest for knowledge that can be brought back to the students and the community.

Sabbaticals are a benefit that cause much discussion in Waldorf schools. Generally given after a minimum of eight years of teaching, sabbaticals are structured in various ways in different schools. Often asked questions include:

• Will a teacher on sabbatical receive full or partial compensation during the sabbatical?

• What are the school's expectations of the colleague on sabbatical? Is it being provided for purposes of personal growth and study, to provide a recuperative period, as a bonus that will allow a teacher to make up for years of low pay by working through the sabbatical year, or to enable a teacher to make a contribution to the movement?

• Is the school making a commitment to rehire the colleague at the end of the sabbatical period?

• Is the sabbatical an automatic benefit after eight years of service, or are there other criteria that control when and how a sabbatical can be given?

• Is the sabbatical being offered in lieu of retirement or severance pay?

At some point in a colleague's relationship with the school, thoughts will turn inevitably to planning for retirement. When it's time for someone to be "put out to pasture," the school does not want to be in the position to tell a colleague, "and buy your own pasture." Instead, the school should be working as a conscious partner with the teacher throughout her years of service, so that her needs continue to be met when she can no longer be of service to the school in the same way. This can be supported by providing a 403B plan which enables the school to make contributions to the retirement fund on both a matched and unmatched basis.

Developing the proper balance of elements in a school's compensation work requires continual consciousness and ongoing hard work. The more that a school is able to project its finances into the future, the better it will be able to understand the implications of decisions that are being made in the area of compensation and plan appropriately for needed changes and expansion.

In addition to multi-year planning, a constant interchange of ideas and information between the faculty, the parent body and the Board is critical for long term health in the area of compensation. This is an area in which it is vital that the Motto of the Social Ethic* ring most true:

> The healthy social life is found
> When in the mirror of each human soul
> The whole community finds its reflection,
> And when in the community
> The virtue of each one is living.

---

* Given by Rudolf Steiner to Edith Maryon, inscribed in a book *The Threefold Social Order*, November 1920.

Chapter 15

The Top Line:
Tuition, Tuition Assistance, and Collection

by

Lynn Kern

The financial health of a Waldorf school community begins with the very first line on the income statement—tuition. Tuition is the primary source of funding for Waldorf schools in America and is directly tied to the educational program the school offers to the community.

What Does Tuition Cover?

Tuition covers all elements of the core program at the school. These include personnel costs (usually the largest expense at a school), facilities, classroom supplies, outreach and overhead.

Depending on the strategy established by a school, it may also include funds to cover capital expansion for new buildings and equipment. Some schools choose to cover these items separately through fundraising activities, rather than building them into the base tuition.

Fees are those items in addition to tuition that are generally unique to a particular child or family. Fees may cover such items as musical instrument rentals, extra-curricular sports fees, curative sessions such as extra lesson or therapeutic Eurythmy, trips and specialized supplies for elective classes.

Tuition Philosophy

When a school establishes its tuition level, there are several general philosophical issues which should be considered:

Tuition levels should be adequate to produce a small surplus of revenue over expenses, generally 2% of revenue. This provides the school with a reasonable margin for the unexpected in the year ahead (lower enrollment, surprise equipment failure, unplanned recruitment expenses).

If capital needs are covered by tuition rather than through separate fundraising, tuition must also provide adequate cash for those items.

Tuition levels must be such that the sustainability of the school is reasonably assured.

Salaries are generally the largest portion of the budget. It is vital that these be set at a level which allows a healthy lifestyle in the community in which the school is located. Budgets cannot be balanced on the backs of our teachers and staff; a reasonable standard of living including access to medical care and a provision for retirement are a moral imperative.

Tuition increases should be predictable. It is far preferable to increase tuition levels 2.5% per year than to hold tuition artificially flat for three years and then post an increase of 10%.

When circumstances point toward the necessity of a large increase, parents should be involved early and often in the conversation. Parents have a right to expect professional planning, collection and disbursement of funds and need to hear about significant changes in practice and pricing.

How, When and Who

Tuition for the coming year is best set as early as possible in the current year. Getting an early start provides several important advantages:

If financially significant changes to the program, staffing, fees or services are being contemplated, an early start allows adequate time for research, establishing appropriate partnerships within the school community, and reasonably accurate financial forecasting.

All segments of the school (College, Board, committees and the Parent Association) can be given an opportunity to share their vision of the future and how it may impact the budget in the coming years.

The re-enrollment process for the coming year can begin early, allowing the faculty time to identify and work with classes which may have concerns affecting enrollment and for the Board and College to make necessary adjustments to the budget based on enrollment.

The timeline used by one established school is:

October	begin top-down, big-picture budget process
November	finalize tuition and fees
December	print re-enrollment documents and related material
January	mail re-enrollment package to all families
February	complete re-enrollment process, begin detailed bottoms-up budget process

It is very helpful to project expenditures in all major categories for several years into the future. This allows priorities to be established and implemented over time as enrollment grows and tuition levels increase. It also makes clear where tuition levels need to be over time, allowing larger increases to be smoothed out over a period of a few years and parents to be partnered early on if necessary. Budgets that are built by looking backward and then adjusting them to meet various changes being experienced in the moment allow the school to get very sleepy financially. Instead a zero based budget that is recreated each year and that looks several years into the future awakens the imagination, allowing for the art of administration to support the physical incarnation of the spirit of the school.

As a reasonability check, compare the school's tuition levels with that of other schools in the market. If a school's tuition is significantly above or below the market level, it is vital that a school try to understand why this is so. Tuition levels that are too low may lead to difficulties with the viability of the school over time, or require that faculty serve at inadequate salary and benefit levels while parents are required to spend their valuable volunteer hours on the basic operation of the school. Schools should not be afraid to set higher tuition levels and then offer accordingly higher levels of tuition assistance. Note that a 10% increase in both tuition and tuition assistance produces an increase in net tuition. This approach can maximize both the revenue and enrollment.

Conversely, tuition levels that are slightly higher than market levels may reflect accurately the fact that a full Waldorf curriculum is both labor and material intensive. This can be easily explained and, when coupled with an appropriate level of tuition assistance, should not affect enrollment adversely.

The tuition setting process should include as broad a cross-section of the school community as possible. If something radical (something new, something big) is being considered it is vital to involve parents early and often.

Payment Schedules and Collection Strategy

For many years Waldorf schools in America have typically employed a monthly payment strategy which has the first payment due in August and the final payment due in June. This schedule was created as a result of several things:

- Schools which do not finalize their re-enrollment process until late in the year have difficulty producing bills in time to accommodate an earlier payment schedule.

- There is a belief that parents won't pay until just before school begins.
- A presumption exists that a significant portion of the parent body will have trouble paying tuition, and that two months are needed without a scheduled payment to allow a catch-up period on delinquent tuition from the prior year.

In the experience of the author, it is far sounder to require a first payment beginning July 1. While it does require that a school complete its re-enrollment process early in the spring so that bills may be produced sooner, it provides several real benefits. Schools have significant expenses during the summer months, including payroll, rent, maintenance and the purchase of all necessary supplies to begin school in September. Unless a school has a large cash surplus from prior years, it will need to find other sources of cash to cover these expenses. Loans for this purpose may be expensive (when they are available at all) and community members who agree to provide financing may do so at the expense of other gifts they might provide to the school. Parents can easily understand the real nature of these expenses and are willing to support the school when they are partners in the school's process.

Often what is described as an unwillingness to pay until school begins is a euphemism for, "I haven't really decided if my child will attend the Waldorf school next year." If these difficulties are discovered early in July, there is still time to work with the family to resolve their concerns prior to September. When concerns are not discovered until school is about to begin, there are often inadequate time and resources to resolve the issues happily. Parents may have already made financial commitments elsewhere, and the back-to-school workload may cause a school to question whether it is willing or able to provide the resources necessary to work through the family's concerns.

When payments begin in July, parents make their first three payments by September when school is beginning. If payment difficulties emerge later in the year, this provides a cushion of time in which the tuition account can be returned to a current status. As the family has paid "ahead," if it should be necessary to dismiss a student after 90 days of delinquency the school will have realized payments roughly equal to the time the student has been at the school.

It is still possible to provide a two month catch-up period when payments begin July 1. In this case the final payment will then be due April 1, ten months after the first payment was due. However, it is important that a school examine the number of families that truly need a catch-up period, versus the benefit to the whole community of smaller monthly payments throughout the year. If a significant number of families fail to meet their tuition obligations, this may indicate inappropriate grant levels in the tuition setting process or a lack of focus and follow through in the area of collection.

Some schools offer parents who pay in full at the beginning of the year a discount on the tuition. This grew out of the practice of delaying billing until August and reflects a school's real need for cash in the summer months. While this practice is appropriate if it reflects the real cost to the school of securing needed cash from other sources, the substantial discounts often associated with these plans can cost the school significant funds. It seems far healthier to ask all families to pay earlier than to offer large discounts to those families with greater financial resources. The savings generated by reducing or eliminating these discounts could fund programs important to the school or make more aid available to those families with need.

Tuition Insurance

Schools and their families should view enrollment as a commitment for an entire year. Contracts should reflect the fact that payment of the full year's tuition is required, and that no credit will be given if a student withdraws or is removed for cause mid-year.

To support this policy, schools are strongly encouraged to offer tuition insurance to their families. This program pays a portion of the tuition for the remainder of the year should a student withdraw mid-year.

Families paying by the month should be required to use this service; it should certainly be offered as a service to families paying in full up-front.

These programs are available through outside insurance providers, or can be self-administered by the school. When something unexpected occurs, it can make things far more pleasant for all concerned when a family doesn't have to pay for services it is no longer receiving. Of course this service also allows schools to budget their tuition levels with reasonable confidence that the funding provided through initial enrollment levels will continue throughout the year.

Tuition Assistance and Adjustment

An important part of life in a Waldorf school is the manner in which the school reflects the threefold nature of its being. These three aspects are commonly seen as the cultural/pedagogical sphere, the rights sphere and the economic sphere.

In today's world we commonly equate economic strength with the return generated on capital assets. Yet when Rudolf Steiner spoke of the economic sphere he described it as the realm of fraternity or brotherhood, a realm whose success is measured by its ability to meet human needs. This responsibility is reflected in his stipulation that he would help found the first Waldorf school only if it were open to children of all economic backgrounds. As a result the tradition of making financial awards to families in need has long been a significant aspect of the tuition setting process in Waldorf schools.

The majority of schools, especially the older well established schools, use a fairly traditional model in which tuition closely reflects the cost of the school operation. Tuition levels may be higher in the high school or upper grades than in the kindergarten, but these differences should be the result of actual cost differences. While a few levels may be helpful and appropriate, schools should guard against having too many levels. "Keep it simple" is good advice here.

These traditional tuition models make tuition reductions available to parents through standardized processes. Scholarships are provided to students, often regardless of financial need, based on some established criteria such as academic achievement, athletic capacity or citizenship. Given the Waldorf emphasis on personal development rather than competitive practices, coupled with the lack of grades in the lower school, scholarships are often limited to the high school.

Tuition aid (funded) and tuition assistance (unfunded) are made available based solely on need. Families requesting aid complete a

140

standardized application, describing their financial circumstances and indicating the amount of tuition reduction they require. These applications are reviewed by a group and a determination of eligibility and the level of a grant are determined. The tuition reduction committee often augments its decision making process by sending these applications to an outside service for evaluation.

Tuition reduction committees are most effective when they include members of three areas of the school—teachers, parents and administration. In this way it is possible for a balanced view to be obtained in making grants, one that balances a view of the child with a picture of the school's finances and a sense for what lives in the parent body.

Discretion is a primary virtue for members of a tuition reduction committee. Each member must be able to receive personal and sensitive information and resist all temptations to share it outside of the committee.

While committee members are selected based on their discretion, this ability is not shared by all applicants for tuition reduction, and the news of grant decisions often finds its way into the parking lot or parent community center. Therefore, it is critical that all decisions are made consistently between families, in line with established school policies, and as if the full details of each grant will be made public to the community.

In recent years a growing number of schools have implemented a tuition model called tuition adjustment. In this program the school trains a large number of volunteer teams to meet with every family in the school community. The purpose of this meeting is to engage in a dialogue which builds a mutual understanding of the needs of the school and the ability of the family to support that vision.

The teams have a checklist of items to review with each family, including the school budget. The conversation also includes a discussion of the family's finances, and the family's ability to contribute to the support of the school, both financially and through participation in the life of the community.

The tuition adjustment model has worked well for a few schools. It is interesting to note that these are schools which had struggled with finances for several years and where the community had come together in a very strong way to insist that a different approach to tuition be found.

Given that this is very different approach to tuition management than is found in much of America, it is vital that several elements be in place for this program to be sustainable over the long haul as priorities

141

change and strong personalities join and leave the school community. These include:

- A true desire for financial transparency which has been consistently demonstrated over time in the school's history.

- Strong support and active participation from the College of Teachers or core faculty.

- Appropriate, well managed tracking and accounting systems that follow the grant process in progress, alerting the program managers and participants early on if the adjusted tuition levels will be inadequate in total to support the school.

- Clear guidelines for decision making so that a large number of independent teams can make tuition adjustments in a consistent manner that will be viewed as fair in the community. Tuition adjustment and tuition assistance both require a certain amount of social standard setting, and it is important that a clear understanding exist about the way in which the community views issues such as a stay-at-home parent for middle school age children or the necessity of a power boat or an expensive automobile.

- A well articulated organization structure that provides, in an ongoing way from year to year, for the selection and training of the teams, preparation of the materials and management of the meeting schedule.

- The school should have a history of strong expense management, allowing it to implement social changes which can be financially volatile in a controlled and conscious way.

The School as a Living Organism

The information above may lead one to think that with enough conscious thought and hard work each school will be able to find just the right way in which to set and collect tuition. Unfortunately, what is "right" at any moment is a result of circumstance and situation, and our policies and practices must adapt as circumstances change in the school community.

There will never be one right or best way in which tuition is set and collected in Waldorf schools. Our schools aspire to be more than organizations, they are living organisms that grow and develop over time. Just as human beings evolve metabolically, cognitively and spiritually in the course of life, so, too, do our Waldorf schools. Finding the right mix of financial practices, policies and procedures is a continual process, one that evolves throughout the life of the school.

142

Our financial resources and the care with which we serve as stewards of them are a reflection of the health of our school community. Where properly managed, they support the spirit of the school as it reveals itself in all its beauty and splendor. This then is the financial art, the creative process in which the economic realm truly supports and enlivens the cultural realm in which a free educational institution can live and breathe and grow.

Chapter 16

The Mandate System

by

Cornelis Pieterse, MA.

What follows is my perspective on the mandate system as it may work in Waldorf schools and other not-for-profit organizations. However, the system may in large measure be applied in business settings as well. I make a distinction between a "constitutional mandate" and a regular mandate. A constitutional mandate is one derived from the Articles of Incorporation or Bylaws of the institution. These mandates (job descriptions) usually pertain to the governing bodies and standing committees of the organization and are permanent and multifaceted in nature. A regular mandate is singular in task and limited in duration. This paper describes the nature and process of a regular mandate.

A mandate is primarily used for groups and individuals that have specific tasks to perform and/or decisions to make on behalf of a governing body. The need for mandate systems is greater for larger and, therefore, more complex institutions, and less pertinent to smaller organizations that are still in their early phase of development.

It is not easy for most of us today to truly empower other people to exercise power and responsibility on our behalf. Somehow we feel that if proposals and decisions are not identical to what we would have done, then the institution will suffer irreparable harm and never survive the mistakes. Such is the illusion under which most of us labor. To gradually wean us from this illusion, schools would do well by setting smaller mandates and to practice this process over and over again until the benefits to the organization and to ourselves become evident. We should learn to consciously and freely delegate responsibility to others without taking it back later when it doesn't suit our purposes.

Mandate definition

I define a mandate as an act of empowerment by the leadership groups of an organization to a smaller group or individual to act, research or make proposals on their behalf. Most mandates have a time limit and narrow task. There must be a leadership body (Board, council, College, etc.) that is authorized to formulate and assign or delegate a mandate to a subordinate body (a committee, task force or individual). There is, therefore, always a reporting responsibility from the group or individual that received the mandate to the authorizing body. Standing committees (like Personnel, Finance, and Evaluation) usually act under constitutional mandates and could, in turn, assign singular mandates to others.

Mandate components

An effective mandate must have each of these components clearly described and documented in all cases:

a. Succinct description of the task

I cannot over-emphasize the need for a very succinct and well-documented description of the task. The delegating body would do well to use all the time necessary to formulate and agree on the task. Any short-circuited process or open-ended description will inevitably result in spending much more energy and time afterwards. Write the task down (one paragraph should suffice), read it and re-read it until everybody is crystal clear and in full agreement.

The task usually consists of fact-finding and making proposals or sometimes decision making. A mandate could also be centered around a function, for instance, mediating a conflict.

b. Reporting responsibility

Make clear and document to whom and when and how (verbal or written) the mandated group should report.

c. Time line of when the task and the interim steps are to be completed

A proper mandate has a very specific time for completion. If the ending date is exceeded, then the authorizing body must consent to another targeted completion date. A defined mandate must always have a time limit, usually no longer than a year in duration. A limited time frame and scope of the task helps in finding qualified individuals to serve with energy and commitment.

d. Criteria for membership and term of service

It should be clarified and documented who are eligible to serve and the length of time of service. Volunteering for key positions is usually not helpful. The group that decides on the mandate should be clear on the general criteria and identify specific people who may qualify. Make this as open a process as possible. Let the light of day shine on this process. When nominating members, specify the reasons why he or she is a good candidate. The candidate has the freedom, of course, to decline. In either case, the nominee should be specific as to why he or she wants to accept the nomination, and also specify the strengths and weaknesses that he or she may bring to the task. Expectations and reservations should be expressed by all sides and, when needed, addressed.

Once the group has been chosen, the team may have a frank discussion among themselves and decide to ask for additional input or clarification. The chair may either be chosen by the mandated group or by the delegating body. How the chair is chosen should be determined when the mandate is formulated.

If qualified members cannot be found, or the same people find themselves serving on many committees at the same time, it may be that the organization is over "committee-izing" itself. This usually happens when (1) groups and individuals are not empowered and entrusted to do work on behalf of the rest and when (2) the leaderships group(s) are confused about their role or lack a common vision. As mentioned above, in this case it is best to start with small pilot projects to practice mandating tasks.

e. Fine-tuning

Once the membership and the task has been agreed upon, the mandated group or individual should work with the mandate in the best way they can and be given a chance early on in the process to suggest amendments, if needed. This is done because there is no substitute for experience gained "in the field." The people closest to the action often gain insights and could make suggestions that may have been overlooked in the original design of the mandate. Walk a fine line between too much rigidity or too much flexibility in amending the mandate afterwards.

f. Process for soliciting input from constituents

It is very important to realize that part of the mandate includes how and how often the group should seek input and information from its constituencies. This is called in-put loops. This is a key element in the process. I would suggest that in most cases the group should be expected to seek at least 2 input loops (depending on the complexity of the task), and submits preliminary proposals for feedback and further input. The constituencies who are asked for input should give it freely without undue expectation that their comments will be incorporated in the final recommendation or decision.

g. Areas of decision making authority (if any) and proposal making

If the mandate includes decision-making authority, we should be extremely clear and have it documented where and how decisions can be made. If this clarity exists prior to granting the mandate, then no one should second-guess or question the decision and outcome. There is nothing more demoralizing and destructive to the people and health of the organization than to undo, second guess, or plainly undermine decisions that were made under a previously agreed upon process. I truly believe that the health and success of an organization depends on how well decisions are adhered to and implemented. Any decision that is later contradicted weakens the life of the organization to the point of paralysis.

In addition, even if a mandated group was only asked to make recommendations, these recommendation should weight much heavier in the debate than the ones that come from those who were not part of the mandate group. When in doubt, or when no clear consensus can be reached, always defer back to those who did the research and legwork on the issue.

h. Evaluation

It is only after the task has been completed and the completion date has been reached that a detailed evaluation of the task and the people who performed it should be undertaken. The mandated group should be asked to do a self-evaluation and look at all aspects of their work: process and outcome. It is in the evaluation that all parties will learn the most. It is here where we can learn how to refine the process and the methodology of the mandate system for the next task. It is at this time that constructive questions can be asked why a certain course of action was taken or decision made. An honest and constructive evaluation becomes the elixir for continuous improvement and health. Do not side step this. Document the findings of the evaluation.

But above all, celebrate the accomplishments and the mistakes, the people who had the power and wisdom to delegate responsibility, and the people who were willing to assume it!

In summary, a mandate consists of the following elements:

Succinct description of the task.
Reporting responsibility.
Time line of when the task and the interim steps are to be
        completed.
Criteria for membership and term of service.
Fine-tuning the mandate.
Process for soliciting input from constituents.
Areas of decision making authority (if any) and proposal making.
Evaluation.

The author would like to thank Kathy Kelly and Herb Walsh, both members of the Lemnis Conference Series coordinating group, for their helpful input.

Chapter 17

Working with Conflict

by

Cornelis Pieterse, M.A.

Conflict is an integral and important part of all social interactions, whether this be in a group setting or between individuals. Waldorf schools, and those of us who work in them, are not immune to this fact. We may often have the experience that conflict finds its way into our faculties and school communities with particular intensity and persistence.

This article was written to address the question of conflict in Waldorf school communities, and also for those groups and individuals working out of an inner connection and commitment to Anthroposophy. At the core of each of these professional communities stands a group of people who have made this inner commitment not only to Anthroposophy, their profession and their respective institutions, but also to each other as colleagues. In most Waldorf schools, a College of Teachers assumes this special responsibility. However, these thoughts and guidelines on conflict apply to any working group that shares a common task.

In working with conflict, and trying to resolve it, we must be clear that there are no rules, models or easy steps to follow. Each situation is unique and demands our full attention and awareness so that we may come to an appropriate response. We are asked to create anew from our inner resources rather than what may be prescribed by social norm or authority. Often we may not know if our actions and solutions are correct for a given situation until we have tried, even experimentally, and then consciously evaluated the results. New soul/spiritual capacities are slowly and tentatively surfacing in humanity! We may already experience that a colleague or school community member can offer a particular insight or intuition, or can exercise a particular social skill that brings healing to a situation. Let's stay awake to what others can bring. We must also learn to recognize and trust our own intuitions and perceptions and have the courage to act out of them.

This chapter explores aspects of the nature of conflict and the role it plays within the structure and development of social life. We will examine our own relationship to conflict (including a few words on conflict and karma) and offer possible guidelines and techniques on working with conflict. We will conclude by describing some exercises that schools can employ to help work with differences.

The Nature of Conflict

With a couple of possible exemptions, the nature of conflicts in a Waldorf school is essentially similar to what we might find in other organizations. We are living in a necessary phase of our human development in which the strongest anti-social forces are at work. Name a shortcoming, and I can find its echo living in my own being! We can all elaborate on our own countless human qualities which stand in the way of a healthy social life: martyrdom, all kinds of fears and phobias, jealousies, prejudice, dogmatism, want for power and influence, to name a few. We also have the basic human needs to be accepted and recognized by others. These legitimate human needs are alive and well in most of us and, therefore, in our communities.

Rudolf Steiner pointed out that sympathy toward a person can be just as destructive as antipathy. An overly sympathetic relationship with another person can hinder a clear assessment of what is helpful or not helpful in a given situation. Seeking to exclusively affiliate with colleagues whom we like may result in cliques and power blocks, which exacerbate conflict.

It is interesting to note that some conflicts have an icy-cold, below the surface, quality. These conflicts tend to run over a long period of time and often find no resolution at all. They are unspoken, invisible, but ever-present and could be described as cancerous in nature. Other types of conflicts explode in the heat of battle, are often short-lived, but tend to recur in definite patterns.

Exercise

To familiarize yourself with your relationship to conflict, make a self-assessment of what type of conflict you tend to "favor," and what type of conflict seems to come to you from others.

The nature of conflicts has an added dimension in Waldorf schools and other organizations that have a strong ideological foundation. We have been entrusted with insights from Anthroposophy about the conditions for human development, coupled with a spiritual, social and economic idealism. Any idealism, no matter how altruistic, can be the source of an overzealous attitude toward life in general and other human beings in particular. To the extent that we allow this content of Anthroposophy to be merely assimilated by our intellect (and thereby remain abstract), and less a matter of daily practice in humility and tolerance, it can be used as a socially destructive weapon. We can justify all kind of opinions and judgments against our fellow human beings, in order to project a position of power or superiority over others.

We need to mention these things not just to wallow in the negative qualities in us, but to clearly acknowledge that they are operative in conflict situations. If we hope to understand and work with conflict in a conscious way in our schools, it is a prerequisite that we are awake to these ever-present antisocial forces. I believe that our times require this awareness of us. If we are not awake, or if we try to ignore or deny the existence of these tendencies, then we make ourselves more vulnerable to their influence!

The weaknesses of the Waldorf movement are also its strengths! Rudolf Steiner was very deliberate in his intention to not have a headmaster or headmistress, or install other hierarchical structures and orthodox social norms for people to fall back on. This fact brings with it, however, that the deliberating and relationship building processes can be much more laborious than otherwise might be the case, and that differences of opinion and conflict will more easily rise to the surface.

Some Psychological Dimensions of Conflict

The chance for a conflict to escalate is greater when we ignore or avoid the conflict.

The more we are emotionally or materially dependent on another person(s), the greater the chance for conflict. In other words, conflict usually occurs within the context of interdependency.

Two people in conflict often share those negative character traits which they perceive and then proceed to criticize in the other. It is a somewhat cruel irony that I will seek to find those people who will best represent character traits that I am determined to avoid seeing in myself. This phenomenon is called "projection."

Differences become conflicts when they are accompanied by emotions. Concepts and ideas do not create conflict. In my experience, strongly expressed intellectual arguments are often thinly disguised but potent emotions. Fear of the unknown and loss of control are possibly the greatest sources for creating and maintaining conflict.

Another irony (life seems to consist of irony and paradoxes) is that conflict provides for greater energy in the group. Intellectual processes, while necessary, tend to dull human consciousness and often creativity!

Exercise

When you are in strong conflict with another person, find a quiet time during the day where you identify the main qualities he/she possesses that bring you into conflict with that person. Then, in an honest self-evaluation, assess what you have in common with that person.

Purpose

This exercise gives a greater understanding of yourself and the other, which may lead to greater acceptance of yourself and seeing the humanity again in the other.

The Role of Conflict

At the end of Scene Ten of the Mystery Play, "The Soul's Awakening" by Rudolf Steiner, we find the dialogue between Lucifer and Benedictus (Johannes' spiritual teacher and guide) concerning who shall have dominion over Johannes' soul—Lucifer or Johannes himself:

Benedictus: "He will admire you but not succumb to you."
Lucifer: "I mean to fight."
Benedictus: "And fighting serves the Gods."

This dialogue may serve as an indication about the role of evil in life. While we should be careful not to automatically equate conflict with evil, conflict certainly has an affinity for the dark or shadow sides of man. And, as in the case of evil, it plays an essential and, therefore, a potentially positive role in our own development and that of our institutions. It is often out of conflict, chaos or doubt that new impulses can enter our social creations.

In the unfolding of a meeting, all of us can confirm the experience when, after a difficult moment—going through "the eye of the needle" by means of a confrontation—the meeting can reach a deeper level of significance. Once that happens, everyone knows it and is inspired by it. The meeting becomes more efficient without losing the necessary depth of deliberation. The analogy of a thunder storm comes to mind, in which the lightning, rolling of thunder, threatening clouds and the driving rain will send us to seek shelter. But how refreshed and light the world feels afterwards; something has been cleansed and renewed!

To recognize, allow for, and process the expression of conflict and differences among members of a group has many benefits. It provides a healthy diversity which will energize all members of a group. It allows for much greater individual and group learning and growth. A faculty, Board or committee will gain greater flexibility and adaptability to meet the ever increasing demands placed on Waldorf schools: the changing needs of the children, curriculum, community life, parent expectations and other social and organizational questions. Through our differences a more meaningful unity and connection can arise with a sense of purpose. Individual contributions, pertaining to the life and performance of the group, are recognized as being essential to the success of the whole group.

Without conflicts we would fall into blissful but dulling sleep. Among other things, conflict awakens us: it calls us to consciousness. This may be one reason that some school communities appear to be addicted to conflict! Maybe it is because people intuitively sense that conflict raises consciousness. Or it may be that staying in conflict enables the community to avoid working on other pressing issues, or even greater conflicts.

If conflict awakens us, we may extrapolate that the more conscious we are as human beings, the less life's circumstances are truly experienced as conflicts. In other words, we still recognize the difficulties in life, but they are experienced as opportunities and gifts. As a life-long process, we slowly gain a different inner relationship to what we used to call conflict.

> The gloom of the world is but a shadow
> Behind it, yet within reach, is joy.
> There is radiance and glory in the darkness.
> Could we but see—and to see, we have only to look.
> I beseech you to look!
> Life is so generous a giver but we,
> Judging its gifts by their outer covering,
> Cast them away as ugly or heavy or hard.
> Remove the covering and you find beneath it
> A living splendor woven of love, by wisdom, with power
> Welcome it, grasp it, and you touch

The angel's hand that brings it to you.
Everything we call a trial, a sorrow, a duty,
Believe me, that angel's hand is there.
That gift is there, and the wonder of an
overshadowing presence.
Our joys, too: be not content with them as joys.
They, too, conceal diviner gifts.
                    - Fra Giovanni (1386-1456)

Conflict and Karma

Living with thoughts about karma and reincarnation may strengthen the main ingredient in all conflict resolution, our inner development! When considering questions of self-development, karma and social life, we must first learn to live with apparent contradictions. On the one hand, for instance, if we know that conflict has a very important role to play, we must learn to accept it and embrace it. Do not reject or fear conflict. We must learn to see and trust that everything that comes to us has a reason and purpose designed to further our individual and social development. These are my core values.

On the other hand, it is very important that we must never seek conflict or, even worse, create conflict on purpose! Life will flow and take its own course. When we are ready (and not before that time), we will meet those difficult experiences that need to come our way.

Perhaps the central contribution by Rudolf Steiner to the spiritual legacy of mankind is his spiritual research into the questions of karma and reincarnation. Never before to my knowledge has any person articulated this spiritual reality so thoroughly and explicitly. From his works we can gain important insights that can shed a unique light on our topic.

Most events and people whom we meet in life, and the general circumstances in which we find ourselves, are a result of our own deeds and experiences in past incarnations. We know this to be called individual karma. One of the implications of this insight is the fact that the difficulties we encounter in other people and events do not find their cause in these people or events but, ultimately, in ourselves. There are no innocent adult victims. Each and every one of us is in control of our own reality. We have options at any given moment. When we blame our problems and conflicts on the people or circumstances (accidents, for instance), we point in the wrong direction. This is somewhat analogous to a young child who, after running into a chair, blames the chair for his pain.

We often hear ourselves say, "If only this person or this particular conflict were not part of our school, the school would be so much healthier, and we could proceed with our tasks." There is a tendency in us to want to surgically remove a problem and to view it as extraneous to the flow of life rather than embrace it. I believe it is an illusion to think that the "other person" is the problem. The events and people in our lives are brought to us by spiritual beings who work in close conjunction with our higher self. How often does it not happen that we encounter the same patterns and the same kind of people and conflicts? We are drawn like a magnet to those people who seem to present us with our issues and dilemmas. These people are mere vehicles for our growth and development on earth. As the child learns to orient himself spatially, congruent to his awareness of the separation of material objects and his own body, we need to orient ourselves in karmic laws. One of these laws tells us that all events coming toward us from "without," are intimately connected with our ego identity and its individual phase of development.

This consciousness needs to grow into a strong inner conviction that recognizes our inner relationship to the difficulties that come our way. As Johannes Tautz phrases it, "We ourselves have sought these difficulties. Man fashions his own destiny. The difficulties that he encounters are his own 'I' mirroring itself in his surroundings, in his social environments."

Considering the unfolding of our destinies, we live within an amazing twofold dynamic. On one hand is the pole of our daily waking consciousness. The world of the senses enters our consciousness, and we are aware of how we think and feel about ourselves and others. In response we make decisions about—and we have preferences for—career, people, lifestyle, goals and values, etc. On the other hand is the pole of our will-life that leads us through our limbs to events and people without our conscious participation and choosing.

Exercise

We need to prepare ourselves so that when a person brings us a conflict, our inner reaction will be of great and genuine interest in that human being. Can we later recall all the details of that moment in the day: the room in which the conflict took place, the people present, colors, clothing, mood, the seating arrangement and sequence of events? We must paint a picture before our soul of everything that was part of that moment. This effort allows us to cultivate an appreciation for the mystery of life and, according to Rudolf Steiner, orient ourselves toward a better understanding of our personal karma.

What often is called "bad" or "old" karma between two people is, I think, a misunderstanding. Karma leads us to the moment of the encounter; then choices and new possibilities enter and weave into the relationship together with what is already given and predetermined. To inwardly turn one's back from a long-standing conflict with another human being by dismissing this conflict as "bad" karma is a subtle form of abdicating one's responsibility toward the present reality of the relationship. I believe that personal karma is not only designed to have us repay old "debt," but has within it fertile seeds for future possibilities and the call to develop new capacities of soul. The complexities of karmic relationships are such that the entire context of one relationship is a mix of negative and positive experiences, all interwoven and indistinguishable from each other.

Elements and Objectives in Conflict Resolution

The following elements and prerequisites are not placed in order of priority of importance. All these objectives should live in our consciousness as we work with conflict. They are applicable if you are a party in the conflict, or if you serve as an outside facilitator.

There cannot really be a question of fully "resolving" a conflict. Some elements in conflict dissolve naturally while others may lead to the next level of challenges in the future. Our first objective in approaching conflict resolution must be to "unlock" a situation so that *movement* can be brought in the fixed perceptions that people have of each other and of issues. If this movement can take place, conflict becomes a dynamic force for change and development.

The second condition is that the *process* of resolution is as important as the end result. In other words, how we go about resolving is more important than resolving an issue. It will be in the process that the necessary learning and social skill-building will occur. It is a common misconception that conflict resolution must result in having the parties smile at each other again and shake hands. While this objective can be an important step, the ultimate purpose of our work must be that paralyzing conflict can turn into creative difference and constructive diversity in our schools. Without diversity, our organizations and human relationships turn stale and stagnant. After all, there can be twelve legitimate points of view to each issue. How can these views be part of our deliberations without mutually excluding each other?

In resolving conflict, we must simultaneously work with two additional and seemingly opposing objectives. One very important goal is to create an atmosphere of *trust* among the parties, to have people look at each other with renewed eyes. The exercises in this chapter are designed to accomplish this trust and to have each party "walk in the shoes" of the other. Without this basic level of trust, we cannot constructively work with conflict. The majority of our efforts will be spent building this foundation.

In the process of building trust between people, it is very easy to by-pass our fourth objective. When we're making progress toward having people trust each other, it will be very tempting to think that now we have resolved the conflict. Often this is not the case. Most important is the pivotal rule that the conflict must be articulated and fully described. In other words, the conflict must become *perceptible*! Perceptible—not only in its effects (because, most likely, the effects are painfully clear to all)—but we must learn to phenomenologically describe the nature and chronology of the conflict. Similar to a faculty's child study, we must describe and study the "biography" of a conflict. This process will have a very important benefit. By making perceptible what was hidden, we externalize and thereby objectify it! Invariably, the conflict loses its destructive grip on the parties. In many cases, the process of bringing the conflict to our consciousness by describing it will be sufficient to allow for sufficient resolution.

The fifth condition is to have the *will* to find a solution! While conflict can inflict great misery on all parties (sometimes for long periods of time), people may still be reluctant to seek a resolution. There can be many reasons for this reluctance. Resolution brings with it the necessity for change and for more work on the part of all members in a group and more accountability to oneself and others. It may, therefore, feel safer and more convenient to stay with the status-quo of existing power structures.

When asked to facilitate conflict resolution, it is very important to assess how committed the parties are to finding a resolution. There are various ways to assess this commitment. We must pay attention to what people say or, more importantly, pay attention to their actions. What is the mood in a meeting? How genuine is the level of exchange and self-disclosure? How willing are the parties to commit to extra meeting time and allot the necessary material and human resources to the process? Do people show up late for meetings. Do they "forget" important agreements? Does another conflict suddenly take precedence? On a subconscious or deliberate level, individuals and groups can be ingenious in avoiding dealing with the issues at hand. It is important not to underestimate the elements that can stand in the way of conflict resolution.

Intimately connected with the "will" to find a resolution is the sixth condition of *courage*. In working with conflict, we inevitably are confronted, not only with the shadow side of the other person, but also with that of ourselves. A precondition for working with conflict is that we don't place ourselves above the others in the conflict. Any sentiment that make us feel that another person's problem couldn't be our own works against the process of resolution. Honest and heart-felt humility joined by a certain "fearlessness" are all essential ingredients.

A seventh attitude is not to seek fault with a person or to find one party "right" or "wrong" in a situation. We must be *non judgmental* in all respects and in everything we do. Invariably both (all) have played their part in the conflict. By drawing sides or pronouncing opinions and "explanations" we invariably add to the conflict. We should be very careful to delineate between the processes of conflict resolution and that of evaluation. The latter aims for a decision or corrective action of some sort. The former, however, is purely designed to accommodate communication and further development.

The eighth requirement is to honor the *freedom* of the other human being. If we recognize that each conflict finds its origin within the souls of the individual parties to the conflict, then resolution must start with accepting our own responsibility in the conflict. We must know that no matter how obvious the shortcomings of the other may be, or how radically wrong his thinking is, I have only the power to change myself. No amount of effort on my part can make me change the other person or have him learn the lessons that I think life is teaching him. The idea of honoring the unequivocal freedom of the human being, so central to the impulse of Anthroposophy, must permeate all our feelings and actions.

Two final guidelines are extremely important to remember and to apply whenever we can. One is that, when we are speaking of human interaction, colleagueship and, especially, difficult relationships, it is important that we learn to speak for our feelings and personal needs. It is a mystery and somewhat a contradiction to me that a movement which excels in enriching the experience of childhood to many, many thousands of children, that we, as adults, are so awkward and suspicious of expressing our feelings to each other. In our frailties and striving we bear "witness" to our humanity again! This brings us to the ninth requirement: *speak from the heart* in anything you say. Be authentic. Conflict will evaporate when we make ourselves vulnerable to the each other, when we can confidently speak from our own strengths, while allowing others to help us with our weaknesses.

The last condition concerns group work. In the vast majority of cases, a conflict between two members of a working group (for instance, a faculty) will adversely effect the workings of the entire group. This particular conflict will live in the consciousness and become the burden of the group. Additionally, almost without exception, other members of the group will find their alliances to the conflict and subsequently contribute to it. For these reasons, resolution should always take place within the context of the *full group*! The benefit to this approach is simply that other members can become co-responsible for the process, and when resolution occurs, its redemptive influence will permeate the group and the entire organization. Please resist the temptation to have conflicts resolved in the corners, so-to-speak, of our organizations.

We now can summarize some of the elements and goals that must be present, as necessary prerequisites, to help resolve conflict:

> Conflict is intimately connected with our biographies.
> Conflict is closely related to our path of inner development.
> It is best to "embrace" conflict and not see it as extraneous to life.
> "Unfreeze" the opinionated perceptions we carry of ourselves, others and issues.

Needless to say, trust is a key ingredient to resolving conflict. Trust, however, does not appear by its own accord. It can only be established in small steps made by both parties.

Make conflict perceptible. When conflict is "named" and articulated in terms of the main issues and chronology of events, then the group has a realistic chance to work with conflict.

Assess whether the parties have a true commitment to resolving the conflict. Listen not only to what people say but also assess their commitment to allocate precious time and other resources and their ability to keep to agreements.

A willingness to work with conflict takes courage by all parties. Resolving conflict often means a departure from the comfortable *status quo* by entering uncharted territories. Professional relationships may have to be re-defined, new obligations undertaken, and/or organizational structures redesigned. Uncertainty often accompanies communities that have a willingness to experiment with new ideas and social forms as part of processing conflicted situations. The collective maturity of a school community is commensurate with how much it can tolerate uncertainty and paradox.

Be nonjudgmental to a fault! Judgments only beget more judgments. Opinions beget more opinions. Who is willing to break this cycle of an "eye-for-an-eye"?

Honor the freedom of each fellow human being to do the work that he or she needs to do in his or her time. Only in the most extreme circumstances will this principle interfere with the healthy running of a school.

Never, never assign the fault of a difficult situation to one person or group. In human relationships, causality is circular. Any attempt to work back to the source or cause of a conflict will lead you to discover yet another condition that proceeded it, ad infinitum.

Learn to speak from your heart and be authentic in all your communications with your colleagues.

Resolve conflicts within the full circle of human beings who are affected by and contribute to the conflict.

Steps

This outline of steps in conflict resolution is much more a general guide than a rigid formula. When we facilitate or directly engage in confronting a conflict, our intuitions will guide us through the process. Very often, individual steps may have to be by-passed, or it may be sufficient to just cover a couple of these "check points." To better illustrate these steps, we will assume that the conflict has escalated substantially, affecting various individuals and different levels of the organization.

1. Assessment and Commitment Phase

This first stage is important because it will lay a foundation and set a tone for the entire process. Primarily, we are considering three interrelated steps. First, there must be an acknowledgment and identification of the "problem" or conflict, including the individuals who may be involved. Usually, by this time, everyone is aware of the problem, and the need for finding a working solution becomes urgent. Second, some kind of an assessment is made about how the problem should be resolved. Decisions are made on how to approach the difficulties. It may just be that two individuals should get together and "talk it out," or that existing channels of communication and/or procedures should be followed; or it may be decided that a third party should be brought in (from inside, or outside the school community) to facilitate the process.

Third, whatever the decision is, the main parties to the conflict must understand, agree and commit to the process! Without some basic form of agreement among the parties, resolving a conflict is practically impossible. In the latter case, a community might find itself, for the school's benefit, making an evaluative decision, some kind of arrangement that will allow for the continued running of the school. These decisions may run from binding arbitration, a negotiated settlement, or probation, to asking an individual for his resignation. Any of these responses may be legitimate and necessary in certain cases, but it should be remembered that a conflict can easily metamorphose and shift to other areas and individuals in the school community, once the identified individual is removed.

2. Biographical and Descriptive Phase

As mentioned earlier, this phase is crucial. When special care has been exercised to make the conflict fully perceptible, some kind of resolution may already appear. In this phase, therefore, it is our aim to fully articulate what the conflict is and sketch its history. We "map" the conflict. While it is important to achieve clarity in describing the circumstances, do not overload with minute details but, rather, learn to characterize the essence of the conflict. Sometimes this can even be done with an image. In this process, it will become clear where the story coincides and where it does not with people's perceptions and memory. If individuals strongly disagree on the course of events and nature of the conflict, we let these discrepancies stand. These discrepancies are part of the complexity of the conflict. Furthermore, at this stage we concentrate on bringing problems to light, not on solving them. It is a very necessary, often a painful, moment in the process to have all parties experience the severity of the conflict.

3. Perception-Sharing and Mirroring Phase

This phase is truly the heart of the resolution process. Following and interlocking with phase two, phase three focuses on the actual interrelationships between people in the conflict. What are the perceptions that others hold of me? What is the impact of my behavior on others? Are my intentions consistent with my actions? Is what I say consistent with what I truly feel and think about others? (Ironically, many conflicts do not arise out of ill-conceived intentions but mostly out of failure to be honest and straight with others, because we "don't want to hurt their feelings.")

The very definition of conflict is that perceptions we have of each other get fixed, stereotyped and distorted. Even the most caring and humane of us will with ease discard data that contradicts the negative images we would want to hold of a person and cling to those observations that confirm our preconceptions. Of course, what makes it more complicated is the fact that our perceptions and opinions of people are not just based on figments of the imagination; they all have a grain of the truth in them! We could say that the purpose of this phase is twofold: One: to "re-align" our soul forces of thinking, feelings and intentions by means of perception-sharing so that our interactions with people can become three dimensional again, i.e. we learn to express what is truly living in us regarding our thoughts and feelings about a person. (The truth is often less painful than a sugar-coated criticism or innuendo.) Two: by the mirroring or feedback process, we can gradually adjust our reality (self-perception) with the reality other people reflect back to us, thereby allowing the impact we have on others to be more consistent with our intentions.

4. Agreement and Contract Phase

If the conflict resolution resulted in the need to have certain forms of behavior and relationship change, then these changes must be clearly documented and agreed upon. For example, it may be that the parties agree to meet together on a weekly basis for the next three months, in order to facilitate continued contact and communication. Or, it may be agreed upon for each party to "journal" their inner work on the issues surrounding the conflict and exchange these journals with each other on a periodic basis. Or, it may be agreed upon to assign a "speaking partner" to each person. This colleague would function as an unbiased listener and advisor. There are numerous ways to accommodate further support and communication with the parties that are in conflict. All these agreements must be ratified and periodically reviewed. None of these arrangements should run forever. They are merely outer support systems that have a temporary value to assist people in making necessary behavioral changes.

5. Systems and Organization Development Phase

In some cases, part of resolving the conflict requires that changes be made in the organizational structures of the school. It may be the formation of a new committee, or changes in membership, or that certain procedures and policies need to be amended. In extreme cases, it might even happen that the very foundation (vision or mission) of a school is being challenged or in need of "re-vision." Individual development and organization development are reciprocal: the one affects the other. Rudolf Steiner indicated that any human creation reflects the consciousness of that human being and of the times, whether this is in art, science or our institutions. I also believe that our creations influence our consciousness. As a rule, though, it would be a mistake to change the organizational structures first, before (or as a substitute to) working with the interpersonal conflict issues! Many organizations resort to making all kinds of system changes, only to find that these collapse because people cannot work together. The old edict is still true: "Systems are as good as the people who work in them."

6. Review and Implementation Phase

When any decisions are made, then we should be clear who, what, when and how things are to be implemented. It also is important to maintain records outlining the conflict resolution process and results. Somewhere down the road, there may be a need to refer back to the proceedings for administrative and/or legal purposes. At all times, maintain a record of the agreements and decisions and read these back to the group before the meeting stands adjourned.

The *review process* is the most important learning tool that we have at our disposal in group and organization development. In it we look back on our agreements and assess what worked well and what did not. Some of the guidelines regarding conflict resolution pertain to the review process as well. A properly conducted review neither judges nor intellectualizes. It merely describes and characterizes, in images, what transpired from a detached but living point of view. Do not fall into the trap of continuing your discussions and arguments. Make the review brief (7 minutes); just a couple of observations and descriptions will suffice. Stay with your personal learning and insights. Leave others free to discover their own diamonds in the sand. Ask open-ended questions like: What worked best? What worked least? What would you have done differently? When was the most difficult moment in the meeting? What image, fairy tale, weather or landscape did you associate with the meeting? How did you personally contribute to the meeting? Where was the golden moment of opportunity? By means of the review process, organizations and people can engage in a continuous learning cycle and elevate even the most challenging experiences with meaning.

Exercises

What follows are a few exercises and process suggestions in conflict resolution and related trust-building/biography and mirroring/feedback exercises. In each exercise, any number of variations are possible.

1. Have opposing parties, in two's, sit across from each other and draw a self portrait. When finished, each interprets their own picture for the other. Then, for 10 minutes, both articulate what new insights they gained of the other in relation to the experience.

2. Have all parties draw, paint or model an image of the conflict. Then, a general discussion is conducted about the nature of the conflict.

3. Have each participant, silently for him/herself, conduct an imaginary conversation with a person with whom you have a real conflict. The conversation should include a confrontation and what you would say and do in response. After 15 minutes, the participant writes down the essence of the conversation and may share this with the full group. The participant should identify helpful behavior and what was most difficult about the exercise. As an option, the full group could offer helpful feedback.

Trust Building and Biography

1. Have half of the group blindfolded. The sighted people each take a person without sight and guide this person through the building or out through the garden/park/street. The sighted person gives full account of all the obstacles on the way. Next, roles should be reversed. Afterwards, the group shares insights and experiences.

2. All biography exercises are essential for promoting trust. As a guideline, avoid long accounts of a person's life and history. Design specific questions to which people, one by one, respond. Examples:
   a.   Describe your favorite room or place while you were a young child.
   b.   What is your first memory, ever?
   c.   Your first love?
   d.   Describe the first time that you truly felt independent (the world is my oyster).

Mirroring/Feedback

Sender:

Seek permission from the intended recipient.

Address that person directly.

Use "I" statements only.

Never speak for others or from "hear-say," but from personal experience and how you were affected by the recipient's comments or behavior.

Only use very specific, concrete and recent examples.

Do not editorialize, moralize or philosophize; just describe.

Make one statement at a time, after which recipient paraphrases and asks questions for clarification, if needed.

Recipient.

Paraphrase feedback.

Make sure you understand feedback or ask for clarification.

Ask for examples and seek feedback from others to confirm or modify information.

Never argue, defend your position or give reasons. Let what is mirrored live in you.

You are encouraged to seek feedback from others.

You may speak to how you were affected by the exchange: Confused, helped, relieved, angered, supported, etc.

For All Participants:

Share new insights and what you have learned.

Remember that in the exchange, the value systems of both recipient and sender are operative; therefore, do not judge.

Each speaks from personal experience only.

Avoid extreme responses.

Repeat process once or twice more, if needed.

Never have one person continuously sit in the "hot seat," but move the process on to other members of the group.

Further Process Suggestions

When in a difficult phase of a discussion, have one person speak at a time, then afterward, another member of the group paraphrases what was spoken. Then proceed to next point. You can also assign two members of the group to sit outside the circle and have them, periodically,

167

reflect back to the group their observations and further process suggestions. I find it extremely helpful if comments are made directly to a person in the group, rather than to speak into the void of the room.

Concluding Remarks

We have certainly entered a time of the very dramatic changes in the political/social/economic conditions in the world. These changes are accompanied by the most severe conflicts. These conditions only reflect, and are a mirror of, the difficulties we face in our own soul and spiritual development. We can expect these conflicts to intensify as time goes on. To the extent that we are successful in working with these challenges, we may not only serve our immediate school communities but also contribute to a healthy social life in society.

Footnotes

[1] Dr. Rudolf Steiner, Lectures: *Die Soziale Grundforderungen unserer Zeit*, Dornach December 6, 1918, translated by Olin Wanamaker. Rudolf Steiner, *The Challenge of the Times* (The Anthroposophic Press, Spring Valley, N.Y. (1941), pp.119-150.

[2] Mystery Drama by Rudolf Steiner, *The Soul's Awakening* translated by Ruth and Hans Pusch. (Steiner Book Centre, Inc., Vancouver, Canada, 1973) pp. 122-123.

[3] See mimeographed translated lectures by Johannes Tautz.

[4] For general background reading see, Rudolf Steiner, *Karmic Relationships*, vol. I-VII, Anthroposophical Press, Hudson, N.Y.

[5] Rudolf Steiner, *Theory of Knowledge, a Goetheanistic World View*. (Anthroposophic Press, Hudson, N.Y 1975) pp. 102 -103.

(This article was originally published by the Economic Committee of the Association of Waldorf Schools of North America, under the title: "Working Together" 1993.)

CONVERSATION GUIDELINES

by

Cornelis Pieterse, M.A.

"We commonly do not remember that it is, after all, always the first person that is speaking. I should not talk so much about myself if there were anybody else whom I know as well. Unfortunately, I am confined to this theme by the narrowness of my experience. Moreover, I, on my side, require of every writer, first or last, a simple and sincere account of his own life, and not merely, what he or she has heard of other men's lives."

Walden; Or Life in the Woods—Henry David Thoreau

These communication guidelines are primarily written for work groups who have decision-making responsibility. However, these guidelines can also be an essential aid in discussions among large groups of people or in a profound one-on-one conversation. I prefer the term "guidelines" to "rules," because groups and individuals must always use their discretion in how these suggestions best fit the requirements of the moment.

At first these guidelines may appear to hinder the regular flow of a conversation rather than foster it. This is a natural phenomenon when acquiring new skills. Before a skill is fully integrated as a part of an individual or a group, the necessary consciousness and effort required can make it awkward or even frustrating. Have patience and perseverance.

Principle: Apply these guidelines when the issue or decision at hand is any one or more of the following: complex, conflicted, impacting many people (different constituencies), requiring implementation, or working by consensus. Conversely, the guidelines can be relaxed if the group is experienced and functions well or when the matter at hand is of lesser consequence.

I have a few assumptions and values that form the conceptual paradigm for this paper.

1. True communication only takes places when participants are fully transparent to each other in what they do, say, think and feel.

2. The message we intended to communicate must be identical to the message received by the listener. In other words, the intention must be congruent with the result.

3. An effective discussion requires that each participant be fully present and authentic, clear, specific, direct, succinct, unambiguous, speaking from his or her experience and from the heart.

4. Each one of us can only be responsible for our own actions and words, not for those of others.

The first guideline pertains to the seating arrangement for the group: All members of the group should be placed so that eye contact can be maintained. A circle or oval serves this purpose best. Note taking should be kept to a minimum. Minutes should be recorded toward the end of the meeting and only reflect the outcomes of the meeting. A flip chart can be used to help remind the group of important points while the meeting is in progress. The point is that no member should be burdened with constant note taking and thereby excluded from the discussion. Ideally, group members should be so engaged in the discussion as to sit at the edge of their seats for fear of missing one single word.

In a conversation it is very helpful to select one specific person in the group and address your comments to that person. The listener need not respond. This guideline keeps the conversation grounded in personal experience and away from abstractions. The technique is especially helpful when a conversation either overheats or loses all energy. I find that, contrary to my expectations, the rest of the group will pay close attention to the proceeding.

It is always helpful to briefly paraphrase the previous speaker's comments before adding your contribution. This guideline assists with the continuity and deepening of the conversation. Paraphrasing clarifies whether the speaker has been correctly understood. You should also paraphrase when introducing a new topic.

In paraphrasing a speaker must keep the following in mind:
- Paraphrase the main point only.
- Keep your paraphrase succinct and simple.
- Check with the speaker (this could be by making eye contact or verbally) whether the paraphrase is basically correct. If the paraphrase is inadequate, let the original speaker make the correction and then proceed with the discussion. Others in the group may assist you with paraphrasing as long as the flow of the discussion is not compromised and you don't lose your turn to speak.

The overall process should take a minimal amount of time, unless major differences of interpretation come to light. In that case, a decision needs to be made whether the discussion should shift to deal with the differences, or remain on topic.

Speak only from your experience. What you hear from a third party (hearsay)—in terms of experiences, perceptions or opinions—should not be part of a serious conversation in which clarity is paramount. So, too, theorizing, generalizing and hypothesizing takes away from meaningful human communication. Many of our conversations are based on these abstractions. Also, do not represent the experiences, perceptions or opinions of others. We should learn to only represent ourselves. If someone's contribution, other then those assembled, is critically important to the discussion, the meeting should be adjourned and reconvened when all the necessary people can be present.

There are only two possible scenarios when speaking. (1) You can speak from your personal experience, insight, or perception. In this case, you need not authenticate your remarks by calling on the authority and support of others. (2) When appealing to the insights of other people, let them speak for themselves. I often hear the argument that others may not be in a position to speak for themselves or are unable to be present for the meeting. As adults, we need to build strength to stand up for our truth. In a genuine effort to be helpful, we can actually prevent others the empowerment and privilege to find their voices.

Connected with the fourth guideline, always be specific in your comments. There is no exception to this rule. Use recent and specific examples to illustrate your comments. George Sammon (a reporter with *The Washington Times*) said, "Specificity is the heart of credibility." I would add that specificity is a necessary condition for understanding others and for being understood.

Make full use of "I" statements. In the vast majority of cases, it is confusing at best—if not misleading—to use a different pronoun than the one that needs to be applied. Substituting pronouns is one of those cultural idiosyncrasies that seem to dictate that to be direct and transparent is impolite or not sophisticated or too confrontational. The use of the pronouns, "we" or "one," instead of "I," may be acceptable in formal settings but not in group discussions.

Speak early in the discussion about what is important to you.

Principle: The more each member in a group is true to his or her insight and experience, and the earlier each member speaks to this truth, the more effectively the group will function.

Or expressed differently:

The time and energy you spend on avoiding speaking your truth in a group, is always greater than the time and energy you spend on naming what is important to you.

Here are some examples: The room is too warm and stuffy, but no one says a word. Members repeat the same point over and over, but no one calls attention to the pattern. The discussion diverts from the agenda, and no one dares to point this out. People are restless or apathetic, but no one calls for a break. Similarly, it may be that one person is in touch with a feeling of discomfort or anger, but fails to speak to this and opts out of the discussion. (Maybe out of a sense of self-preservation.) If a work group loses even one of its members by non-participation, the group's full potential isn't utilized.

Restrict your comments to one main point at a time. Observing this guideline allows the other group members to stay involved and to participate constructively. This also makes it easier for the next speaker to paraphrase your comment.

To ensure full participation on the part of all members, it may be helpful at important junctures in the discussion, to go around the circle and have each person briefly speak to the question. Another technique, used by Native American cultures, is the use of a "talking stick." Only the holder of the stick has the floor. The conversation proceeds by passing the object around in a timely fashion and to whoever seeks to be recognized.

Ask questions only to seek information. So many questions are in fact rhetorical in nature (meaning, I don't want an answer) or statements in disguise. A genuine question to seek information or to inquire about a troubling situation is always very helpful. However, pay careful attention to how often a question is used for other than informational purposes. If you have a point to make, make it without dressing it up as a question.

About confidentiality and disclosure! Confidentiality is often a loaded and complex issue in a group. The group should make it clear at the end of its deliberations what aspects of the discussion are requested to be held in confidence. In my opinion, the only topics that qualify are those related to personnel questions and non-business agenda items, like personal sharing. Even in the case of personnel issues, your constituencies should be given appropriate updates and requests for input, as long as the lawful rights of the person are not violated. The best use of the concept of confidentiality is the attitude: "I have 'confidence' in you to treat what we have shared in an appropriate manner with those outside our circle." This attitude leaves people free and calls on their highest motivations.

In the vast majority of cases, the demand for confidentiality is overused and often employed—maybe with the best of intentions—to control the legitimate flow of information to others. A good guideline to follow is the answer to the following question: Will our constituencies be impacted in any way by our decision, or by the information we hold? If the answer is "yes," you should disclose, and disclose earlier!

When in doubt, always err on the side of full and early disclosure. The tendency to hold on and control critically important information is widespread in most sectors of our society. I have learned from difficult personal experiences that failure to disclose is poor practice and weakens the trust among those who depend on the organization and on me.

Connected with the above is the use of anonymity. In most, if not all, cases that arise in the course of daily adult interactions, anonymity is highly inappropriate. It flies in the face of being direct, honest, authentic, and for taking responsibility for your actions and opinions. Only in instances when physical safety is at stake (as may be the cases of abuse, or if there is a great differential of power, or when we are dealing with minors) should a person be granted anonymity.

It must be made clear to anyone who seeks some type of action or result from what he or she has shared in confidence, that anonymity can no longer be maintained. If a group opts to act on behalf of an anonymous person, the rest of the community is left with only partial information. This will breed distrust and lack of support.

Of course, when a person seeks anonymity, we should treat the matter with respect, understanding and diplomacy. By providing all the safeguards we can muster, we must then coach the person to a place where he or she can take responsibility for his/her request.

We now can summarize all of the above in the form of an agreement that each one of us can make to our fellow group members. This agreement could be a formal group agreement, or an informal commitment on the part of any of its members. Group members should conduct periodic evaluations to see what adjustments (if any) and additions need to be made to the "contract."

My Commitments to the Group

I will speak to what is important to me (thoughts, feelings, observations) in a timely manner and in a non-accusatory or judgmental way.

I will be direct and specific in all my communications by using recent examples based on my experience.

I will speak from my experience only (not from hearsay or interpretation) and, therefore, speak from the "I."

I will be direct and specific in all my communications by using recent examples based on my experience.

I will speak from my experience only (not from hearsay or interpretation) and, therefore, speak from the "I."

I will paraphrase the main point made by the previous speaker. I will paraphrase especially when there is emotional content, or when I seek clarity, or when I intend to change the subject.

I will not interrupt when others speak.

I will only ask questions for clarification or when I need more information.

I will address my comments to one member in the group.

I will use appropriate self-disclosure to share my feelings and thoughts.

When necessary, I will disclose the assumptions and motivations that underlie my ideas, comments, and actions.

I will actively and in a timely manner solicit feedback from others on my behavior, comments and ideas.

I will only provide feedback after given permission from the intended recipient.

I will honor each member of the group and leave that person free to accept or reject any or all aspects of the feedback.

I will honor confidential information.

I will support all group decisions as my own, whether I was present for the meeting or not.

I will be punctual and honor the meeting times.

I will be comfortable with silence in the group.

Chapter 18

Technology for Administration

by

Agaf Dancy

Waldorf schools and Waldorf teachers have sometimes been viewed as "latter-day Luddites," among the last holdouts for such "dated" skills as handwriting in a point and click world. It is true that we go against the trend in preferring human over machine contact and instruction in kindergarten and the grades, delaying introduction of computer and media technology until the high school years. We have sound pedagogical arguments for doing so. Yet in the administration of our schools we are increasingly recognizing the importance of making full use of the tools available to us through technology. The benefits of computerized record keeping, information retrieval, document creation and communication by fax and email can be significant. The potential for increased efficiency and improved speed and flexibility in responding to the needs of our communities through the use of technology is great. This article attempts to offer advice on how to effectively incorporate technology so as to maximize that potential.

Having said this, I nonetheless tremble at putting any recommendations into print. The hi-tech world is evolving so rapidly that what is said here is likely to be out of date before it reaches its readers. With that in mind, I will try to focus on the more general issues that should be relevant in 2002, while also giving some specific recommendations as they apply to the situation in 1999.

Computer Equipment

When should we get a computer and why? The answer to this question varies in relation to the size of your school and the nature of the tasks to be done. Many things that will eventually be computerized may be better done manually when your school is very small. Maintenance of student records and even parent mailing lists may take less time with paper files and Avery labels when you have just a preschool and kindergarten. Devising a schedule for subjects after morning lesson may be better done with poster boards and post-it notes, even for an elementary school.

Some tasks are significantly improved through technology right from the beginning, however. Correspondence and the production of promotional literature are made so much more efficient and "professional" by use of a computer that it is almost unthinkable to attempt these tasks the "old" way. Budget preparation and financial record keeping are certainly possible for a small school using manual systems, but the use of accepted accounting principles as built into the structure of computerized accounting programs can be a real benefit from the start. For this reason there should be at least one computer available for such functions from the very beginning. As your school grows and the administrative tasks become more complex and time-consuming, the benefits of increased computer usage will soon become apparent in relation to those tasks.

Who needs one?

Basically, in a school past its infancy, everyone who works in the office needs a computer or access to one without having to queue up for long periods. The secretary/receptionist needs to type letters and is often responsible for maintaining various mailing lists and student records. The bookkeeper and business manager need one to manage the accounts, pay bills, generate statements for parents, and manage the budget. The development and enrollment people need to track prospects, generate outreach literature, etc. Teachers need access to one or more, depending on the size of your faculty, to handle correspondence, produce teaching materials and for a thousand other tasks. Smaller schools may have individuals wearing multiple hats, of course. But a good rule of thumb would be to have a computer for every key individual in your administration.

Who will buy, install and maintain equipment and software?

Every school needs a resident geek. If you find some of the terminology I use later in this article to be new or foreign, you're not it. There may be a faculty or staff member with prior computer experience or a parent interested in helping. You may also need the services of a local computer maintenance company to help decide on the right equipment and software. But you should still have someone on your own staff who can deal with outside vendors knowledgeably and can fix some of the smaller problems that arise without having to call in the "experts." Make sure to provide some time in his/her schedule so that this doesn't happen on top of an already full workload. It may be necessary to send one or more people for training (also true of those who will use the software). Often this can be obtained through your local community college at a fraction of the cost of the professional seminars that are frequently advertised.

To Mac or not to Mac—is that the question?

Early in 1998, it was possible to imagine that there would be no more Apple Computer in the near future. Then Apple began to turn around, most notably with the immensely popular iMac, and things look much brighter for its future. Thus, there is no particular reason to choose an IBM-compatible machine over a Macintosh system on the basis of the future of the company. So the real issues are comparable features and price. It used to be clear. Macintosh had a superior machine and a great operating system with a user-friendly graphical interface (those icons and drop-down lists that you point and click on with your mouse) and outstanding software for business and publishing. IBM and IBM clones (Apple only licensed clones for a limited period) were much less expensive. These distinctions have become less significant over time. IBM operating systems such as Windows 95, Windows NT and Windows 98 have begun to be indistinguishable from Macs from the user's point of view. Reliability (especially under NT and 98) has improved significantly. Meanwhile, Macs have finally begun to be priced competitively.

Among the differences that remain: people who do serious graphics and publishing work generally swear by the Macs (though much of the same software is now available on IBM's and is more than adequate for the sort of work a school is likely to do). People who share files (or software) are more likely to find others using IBM-compatible equipment (since 90 percent of the market is in IBM and its clones). In the end, it probably doesn't matter which way you go. You might find that someone in your community could provide access to machines of one or the other type at a discount—or better still, to start you off with a gift. Often it can happen that individuals and businesses who are upgrading to top-end equipment can realize more in terms of a tax advantage by donating their present equipment to a non-profit than they could by selling it. You may also have a good local source for government or university surplus. Or if you do purchase, you might find that one or the other is priced more competitively with respect to your needs. The outcome of these kinds of scenarios will probably be the basis on which you decide.

Whichever way you go, the best advice I can offer is to make your decision and stick with it. Although improvements have been made, files and software are not easily portable between the two platforms, nor is local networking simple. You will find it very frustrating to have both kinds of machines in your office.

How fancy/fast/expensive a computer should we buy?

This is a question whose answer changes with each new version of more powerful software that comes out, requiring more memory and more processing power. Although gifts are a great potential source of equipment, be wary of accepting anything that is too outdated. There is a glut of such equipment that parents and friends would love to donate, but much of it is good for little more than doorstops. There is nothing you can do with a 286 or 386 computer, and little you can do with a computer less powerful than a 486 with lots of memory and at least a 66mh processing speed. Thus, the old saying, "Beware of geeks bearing gifts." If you were purchasing a system, a basic (minimum) configuration to serve your needs now (August, 1999) and for the next few years would look like this:

- Processor: Pentium I or comparable AMD, Cyrix or Celeron at 233mh or better
- G3 or better for Mac
- Memory: 32 Meg or more
- Hard drive: 2 to 4 gigabytes
- CD-ROM: 24X for at least one machine if networked; for each if not networked
- Modem: 56K for at least one machine if networked; for each if not networked
- Floppy disk: 3 $1/2$ inch needed; 5 inch has become obsolete

- Ports: 2 serial, 1 parallel
- Network card (see below)
- Monitor: 14", .28 dot pitch VGA or better

All machines these days come with sound card, mouse and 101-key keyboard.

Machines such as the one described above do not need to be expensive. Shop around, check mail-order and the Internet, and check discounts for schools. At this writing it's possible to find a system such as the one described above for around $600, with monitor. You can also pay three times that amount if you stay with the name brands like Apple, IBM, Compaq or even Gateway and Dell. The advantage with the name brands is strong warranty protection, service and flexibility with respect to upgrading. If I were buying a "high-end" machine that I hoped would last for five or more years (an eternity in computer terms), I might opt for the name brands. However, at the low end of the market, such as the basic machine configured above, price may be the controlling factor—the machine may be "obsolete" after three years anyway. Even low-end machines will generally come with a one-year warranty. In my experience, electronic equipment either breaks right away or else not for a long time.

What about printers?

A printer or printers is the key piece of additional equipment you will need. There is a bewildering variety of equipment available these days, and which item is best for you will depend on your particular situation. For a small office just getting started, the relatively new "all-in-one" machines such as the HP OfficeJet provide multiple functions, (B&W, and color printer, copier, scanner and fax) and save space, all for about $500. They have limitations, though: the copies are not what you'd get from a "real" copier, and you wouldn't want to do more than one or two at a time (which is to say, your office will need a real copier anyway). And though the new inkjets are much better than they were, they still can't compare to a LaserJet for crispness—for $200 more, HP now offers a laser (B&W) version of its all-in-one machine. One such machine can make sense in an office: it eliminates the need for a separate fax machine and provides color printing capability and sheet scanning as well. If you purchase the inkjet variety, you will need at least one other LaserJet printer as well to produce high-quality originals for reproduction. If you are networking and sharing your printers, it pays to consider getting a single higher-end machine—or even to lease/purchase a good copier with network capabilities so that it can double as a printer (see networking below).

Do we need a color printer?

Although they're fun, you probably don't need one (with the possible exception of your PR person). Most of your documents will be copied to many people and will end up black and white anyway. When you're doing things for a color brochure, you can put your color files on disk and send them to your printer, who will get higher resolution than you could in your office anyway. If you choose an all-in-one machine as one of your printers, you'll probably get color printing capability with it for those times when you would like it.

What about brands?

Hewlett Packard has a fair share of the market for good reasons: quality, service, warranty and reasonable price. They're not the only ones out there, however: Epson, Compaq, Panasonic and OkiData, to name a few, make fine machines and should be considered. Compare features and price. Stay away from off-brands and discount brands. I would probably get in trouble naming names, but oh, Brother!

What other equipment do we need?

Your Outreach/PR person would benefit from having a *color flatbed scanner* to copy photos and artwork. Sheet scanners, such as come with the all-in-one machines, are fine, but you don't want to have to rip pages out of nice books to feed them in. 600-dpi resolution is quickly being replaced by 1200-dpi for not much more (in the $300-400 range). That begins to approach true photo quality. All scanners come with OCR (optical character recognition) software that is getting better and better at taking print off a page and making it usable by your word processing software. It's not perfect, but it beats retyping things! You should also have some form of *data backup device,* such as a Zip drive or (for the whole network) a tape backup system. I can't stress enough the importance of having *and using* such a system! Nothing strikes terror into the heart of a serious computer user more than the thought of a hard disk crash and the *loss of all your files,* if you don't have them backed up external to the computer. Iomega (Zip, Jaz and Ditto) is the industry leader in these devices.

Local Area Network

What is a local area network (LAN) anyway?

A LAN is a method of connecting all of your computers in your office, so that each one has access to certain shared resources on the others. It uses a network card in each computer (PCI 10 or 10/100 Base T Ethernet adapter) and eight-strand wire that looks like telephone wire to connect the computers together. Resources that can be shared include files on hard drives, CD-ROM drives and printers. With special software, a modem can be shared as well. There are many benefits to this arrangement:

You can purchase fewer and better printers with the same dollars since several users can share them. There are a number of very good network printers available now. Some copiers also double as network printers, and can be controlled directly from any of the computers on your network. Put the printer next to your coffee machine—that gives you an excuse to get up and chat with your co-workers while waiting for your job to finish!

You can share files. This is especially useful to avoid the proliferation of redundant files—separate, and not equal copies of parent files, student files, financial records, etc. One computer can be designated the "server"—possibly one that is somewhat faster, with a larger hard drive—and can be the physical repository of your commonly shared files. Anyone else can access them from their computer as easily as if they were on their own. In many cases, multiple users can be working with the same files at the same time. You can still have certain files or sections of your hard disk "walled off," protected by passwords so that they are not accessible to others. You will find it amazingly useful, however, to be able to share files with others.

You can speed up interoffice communication. You can set up a local mail server to allow you to post messages to one another and do "broadcast" messages to whole groups, without resorting to slips of paper that so easily seem to disappear. You can "attach" documents or other files to these messages as well. These same benefits can be achieved by setting up Internet email addresses for everyone, but you will probably find it more cost-effective to do it with local email.

How difficult/expensive is it to set up a LAN?

It used to be that you *really* needed a geek in-house if you were going to have a LAN. They were difficult to set up and temperamental. All that has changed. Modern networks use 8-strand wire through hubs rather than coaxial cable, which makes problems much easier to isolate and fix. Operating systems from Windows 95 up provide fairly maintenance-free network functionality (as does the Mac). Windows 98 practically sets itself up. Windows 95 needs a geek to do the initial setup, but then it works just fine for small networks such as you might have in a school office. Windows NT is the Cadillac of network operating systems, but is more expensive and not really necessary for a small office. As to cost, the Ethernet cards for each computer can be had for as little as $15-25 (if they don't come pre-installed in your computer); cable to connect the computers for less than $0.50 a foot; a small hub to connect up to eight computers for around $50-75.

Internet

Why use the Internet?

There's a lot of hype about the Internet. For some lonely souls it turns into a black hole that keeps them surfing well into the wee hours. Discrimination is necessary when evaluating what you find there, as there's no "quality control" about the content. But there is also a vast potential for the movement of information, commerce and communication. When your administrator is shopping for school supplies, computer equipment or cheap airfares, there are good resources on the web that can save time and money. Most useful, in my view, is the potential for communication. With three Regional Chairs, a Publications Chairperson and Trustees at far-flung locations around the continent, we at AWSNA use email regularly (daily) to keep in touch with one another and with many of you at the member schools. Email has revitalized letter-writing and given it the speed of the phone lines, while making communication easy and inexpensive with colleagues in Europe and beyond (we are presently having conversations with friends in China who are interested in starting Waldorf schools there!).

Why this sales pitch?

Because in addition to the benefit I feel it would provide for each school, it would make AWSNA's communications with the member schools vastly more efficient! If we knew that all the schools had email addresses, we could broadcast information (including things like the bimonthly news bulletin, minutes from Delegates' Meetings, announcements about conferences and much more) to the schools within hours, with no postage expense. We could also have meaningful conversations with the Delegates and others about issues we are considering. We could create a restricted chat room or rooms that would also be available to you to network with teachers and administrators in sister schools. Consider the "Fifth Grade Teachers' Chat Room" or the "Development Officers' Network." You could also broadcast announcements of events at your schools and/or post them on bulletin boards or chat rooms. The possibilities are exciting!

How do we connect, and what's it cost?

You need a fast modem (56K is about the limit for ordinary phone lines as of this writing, although local phone lines in some rural areas may not yet support this speed), which hopefully has been provided on the PC you purchased. If not, an internal modem (a card that plugs into a slot inside your computer) can be purchased for $35-50; external modems (a box with a cable that attaches to one of your computer's serial ports) cost slightly more, on average. Either way, they plug into an ordinary phone jack. It's best to have a phone line to use that you don't depend on for voice calls. It's fairly common to share the line you have for your fax machine.

The next thing you need is to set up an account with an Internet Provider (IP) to provide you with access to the Internet and some number of email addresses. An email address is like a post office box—it can be for one person, or it can be shared. If you have just one address, you might have your secretary retrieve the email and then reroute it electronically, via your local email system, or manually by printing it out. AOL, Microsoft Network and CompuServe are well known and provide unlimited access for about $20 per month. You can usually find a local IP to provide similar service for as little as $10 per month. What you choose may depend on which IP offers the best price for the number of separate email addresses you want, and whether or not you want web hosting (your own web home page advertising your school, which interested people could look up). Finally, you need a browser (software to access sites on the web) and email software. Typically, the choice is between Microsoft Internet Explorer 4.0 (with Outlook Express for email) and Netscape Communicator 4.0. Both are fine; both often come bundled with your computer and are often automatically installed if you choose to install AOL or MSN or others. If you go with a local IP, they will probably give you their version of Explorer or Netscape, pre-configured to dial up and connect to their service.

What if we have a local area network?

Modems are not typically shared over a LAN the way other resources (such as hard drives and printers) are. That means that each computer must have its own modem to access the Internet. Fortunately, there's a solution to this. You can install modem-sharing software, such as Artisoft's Ishare, which allows several computers on a LAN to access the Internet simultaneously over a single modem. We use this at the AWSNA office, and it works fine. However, if you have more than five or six computers on your LAN, you may find that things bog down if too many people are trying to access the Internet at the same time. There's a solution to this, but it's more expensive: have the phone company install an ISDN line and connect it to the LAN with an ISDN modem (you will also need to make sure that your IP can support ISDN access). This will easily support as many as 20-30 simultaneous connections. The Rudolf Steiner School of Ann Arbor uses this technology to teach Internet skills to 20 or more high school students at one time. The ISDN modem typically costs from $200-300. The installation and monthly charges for the ISDN line are considerably higher than for regular phone lines, however. Charges vary from place to place, so you will need to research this in your local area. Note: there is a lot of support from the federal government for getting schools online these days, which you may be able to take advantage of in getting the costs of Internet access paid for. Check with your local school district to see what help may be available.

What about a web site?

Many Waldorf schools have already developed web sites to advertise their programs online. AWSNA can provide links to these from its online school list, if you set one up and let us know (just email us a note about it!). Your local real estate agents will want to know about it, also, as many families relocating into your area will be researching the schools ahead of time on the Internet. It's not terribly expensive to have an IP provide you with space for your web site. Design can be simple or complex, artistic or basic, depending on the resources available to you in your community. Chances are, there are parents with web authoring skills who would love to contribute to the school in this way (often they don't get to use their professional skills to benefit the school in other ways). If you have a high school, you can have students contribute to the design and maintenance of the site as well (with supervision, of course!).

Software

Software is the term used for the computer programs that run on your hardware (the equipment). There are basically three types of software. Operating system software controls the physical operation of the computer components and is what initially loads (boots up) when you turn your computer on. Housekeeping software works in tandem with the operating software to monitor your computer's operation while it's running. Application software is what you actually use to perform your tasks. These will be described briefly below.

Operating System software comes preloaded on your computer. IBM compatible machines generally run under Windows 95 or Windows 98 (offices with larger LANs generally use Windows NT). Macs run under their own proprietary operating system, with OS 8.6 the most current version. You will not generally need to change the operating software or do anything to it unless something major goes wrong. At that point, enlist the help of your geek. Upgrades to the operating system are released periodically. Some offer significant improvements, such as the change from Windows 3.1 to Windows 95. Others may be of more interest to the high-end user. You will probably do fine sticking with the operating system that comes preloaded on your computer. When you buy your next computer, it will probably come with the most current system available at that time.

Housekeeping software, also known as utilities, may or may not be preloaded. There are two kinds of utilities that are particularly useful: anti-virus utilities and system/file management utilities. An anti-virus program is essential if you are going to be on the Internet or will be sharing files with others on floppy disks. It's the computer equivalent of practicing "safe sex," and is unnecessary if you remain "celibate." Viruses are computer programs created by anti-social geeks which "infect" files that you may download from the Internet or get on a floppy disk from someone else's computer. They range from annoying to thoroughly destructive. Since there are new ones constantly being created, the only way to maintain protection is to regularly update your anti-virus program's "virus definition files." The leading anti-virus programs provide for doing that automatically every month or so by accessing their web sites and downloading the latest virus definitions.

Norton and McAffee are among the industry leaders for anti-virus software. Norton also provides one of the best sets of general-purpose utilities available—and now also bundles these with its anti-virus progam in a package called Norton System Works (McAffee also provides a similar package called McAffee Office). Both are available for around $100. Among the other useful utilities is DataViz's Conversions Plus, which is very helpful if you share files with others who may have produced them with programs that you don't have. It is capable of translating a wide variety of file formats, including going from Mac to IBM and opening various attachment files generated by Internet applications.

Application Programs serve any number of functions. The most common one is word processing, such as is being used to produce this article. Spreadsheets are used to manipulate financial data and create budgets. Data base programs allow users to manage a variety of interrelated lists, such as student and parent name and address lists, donor lists and other kinds of mailing lists which you will need for communication with parents, recruitment and fund raising. Presentation software can be used to generate fancy presentations and slide shows. Several major software vendors offer bundled "suites" of interrelated software for the most common uses, and this is certainly the best way to purchase them. The leaders in this area include Microsoft Office 2000 (Microsoft Word, Excel, Access, Outlook and PowerPoint), Lotus Smart Suite, and Corel (which is now including sophisticated speech recognition software along with WordPerfect 8). I have a strong preference for Microsoft. Much as we all seem to love bashing Bill Gates, his company seems to keep producing winners. Microsoft Works is a simplified, stripped-down version with similar functionality which many people find easier to learn. I would go for Microsoft Office 2000, myself. Typical prices range from $300 upgrade to $550 full version.

Custom software for Development is generally built around a database, with specialized reports and other functions designed to serve the needs of development. A program called ebase, an interactive database designed for nonprofits, has the distinct advantage of being FREE. Dana Myers (Honolulu Waldorf School Development Director) likes it for its simplicity and flexibility. It may be downloaded from www.ebase.org. There are three programs designed for fundraisers and development officers from JSI: DONOR$, a DOS-based program that is still supported but will be phased out eventually; its successor, PARADIGM, a Windows-based, very sophisticated program; and MILLENNIUM (yes, that's right), that looks like it does everything but give you the money itself. Check them out at *www.jsi.com/frs*. Nancy Trueblood (Chicago Waldorf School Development Director) uses DONOR$ and likes it. You would probably order PARADIGM if starting from scratch (they may not even sell DONOR$ now). Contact JSI for prices, but it probably won't come cheap. One more package, called IntraServ, is available from DMG Corp. Like MILLENNIUM, this product uses very recent technology (it's written in Java, for instance) that assumes you are running a fairly up-to-date computer. DOS-based users need not apply. You can check it out at *www.dmgent.com*.

Blackbaud, mentioned below under General Accounting, offers fundraising software called Raisers Edge (www.blackbaud.com). Donor Perfect is yet another fundraising software package (www.donorperfect.com). Just to confuse you with more choices, there is Donor II, which may be viewed at www.donor2.com. These and many more software products are advertised in the journal "Nonprofits and Technology," which is a very useful resource for fundraisers. The journal has, of course, an online version at www.pj.org.

Publishing software is used to produce sophisticated PR material, presentations, brochures and books. The industry leader here is Adobe, with a stable of products: Adobe Pagemaker, Photoshop and Illustrator (bundled as Adobe Graphic Studio). You may not need all of these unless you're doing full-scale publishing. For many purposes, Pagemaker alone suffices. The other leaders in publishing software are Corel and QuarkXPress. All three sets of programs are extremely powerful and sophisticated, with more features than most of us will ever use. Upgrade prices can be as low as $120; full version prices are around $550.

General Accounting software is a must for your business manager/bookkeeper. There are several good packages at prices ranging from $120 to $300, among them Peachtree and Quickbooks. Both systems integrate functions like check writing, billing, ordering, payroll and budgeting along with a variety of reporting options. Quickbooks Pro 99 ($150 single-user, $300 2-users) gets my vote for network functionality (your bookkeeper and business manager can access the same files simultaneously over your LAN) and its new integration with Microsoft Word and Excel. That makes it possible to do customized mail merge letters to your parents from your Quickbooks customer file, or do financial analysis of Quickbooks data using Excel. The Cadillac of accounting software for nonprofit organizations is probably Blackbaud. It was designed from the start to do nonprofit fund accounting, and it integrates with student billing, admissions and registrar packages—as well as a project, grant and endowment management system. Unfortunately, you need a grant or endowment to be able to afford it. Individual components tend to cost $2000 each, with an ongoing yearly maintenance fee of 20 percent of list.

By the way, even though you can do payroll yourself using Peachtree or Quickbooks, I strongly advise you to also look into using a payroll service such as Paychex, Inc. for a monthly fee. Keeping on top of tax law, withholding and federal and state filing requirements are a highly specialized area full of headaches and potential penalties (the IRS is not especially forgiving). As a middle ground, Quickbooks is now offering an online Payroll service that integrates its software at your local site (for producing paychecks) with its offsite management of tax reporting.

Scheduling/Project Management software may be especially useful if you get involved in a major project such as constructing a new building. Microsoft Project provides for several scheduling formats, such as Pert or Gantt scheduling. Unless you are involved in a complex project such as this, you will probably not need such software.

Other specialized software you might find useful includes Scheduling programs and Registrar/Student Records programs. These are most helpful at the high school level, where such things get complex. There is one interesting package called the Waldorf Transcripts program that has been designed especially for Waldorf high schools to help translate our unusual mix of block and track classes into the more traditional course credits expected by college admissions officers. At present it is only available in a DOS based version. Contact Dianne Phillips, (978) 975-9765, for more information.

Training

Like any other tool, computers and computer software may be used clumsily or with skill and sophistication. It makes little sense to invest significant resources in such equipment and software without making a corresponding investment in training for those who will use the technology. A colleague observed that there are still people on the office staff who use a word processor and hit ENTER whenever they come close to the end of a line of type, as if they were using an older-model typewriter! Without proper training in their use, computers can in fact become a cumbersome waste of time, making tasks more difficult than if they were done manually. There are many sources of training. Community Colleges and extension programs often offer a slate of programs, both on beginning computer use and on particular software packages. Many private outfits offer intensive workshops as well. Go to any computer store and ask for advice on what's available in your area. There are also interactive tutorials available from internet-based companies and combination text plus CD-ROM programs for most of the popular software. In fact, many of the software packages come with excellent tutorials built in. The trick, however, is to discipline oneself to actually sit down and use them. That's where the workshop or course format can be preferable. Regardless of the approach you take, the key thing is to provide the training for any current staff who will use the new equipment or software. When hiring new staff, make sure they already have experience on the software they will be using—or be prepared to pay for their instruction. Anything short of this is a waste of your school's money. *(Thanks to Nancy Trueblood, Chicago Waldorf School for reminding me of the need to emphasize this topic.)*

In Closing

The last ten years have seen remarkable gains in the functionality of computers and computer software, especially with respect to their application to traditional office tasks. The last five years has seen the emergence of the Internet as a potent agent, for good and ill, in commerce and communications. We can expect more dramatic changes, coming even faster, in the years to come. Good voice recognition software is on the horizon and is already becoming fairly functional on the faster machines. Before long, articles such as this will be spoken rather than typed. Computers will respond to voice commands rather than clicks of the mouse. Teachers (and students) will have access to "lunchbox" computers costing not much more than $100 that will be able to do all this as well as access the Internet via radio links.

Waldorf schools can and should take advantage of these tools as appropriate. They can make us more efficient in our daily tasks, leaving us more time for the really important things—the human interactions occurring in the office, the hallways and the classrooms that weave our lives together in meaningful ways. Let us not forget that that's what they're for. Let us not allow them instead to isolate us from one another, beguiling us into accepting surrogates and "virtual" realities in place of true experience and direct interaction. Let us not turn the servant into the master.

About the Authors

Dave Alsop completed his Waldorf teacher training at Emerson College in the early 70's, after which he joined the staff at the Sacramento Waldorf School. During his tenure there, he was a class teacher for six years and then the Administrative Chairman for eight years. In 1988, Dave became AWSNA's first full-time staff person and has served as its Chairman since 1990.

John Bloom is the Gifts and Grants Officer at the Rudolf Steiner Foundation. Prior to that he served as the Administrator for the San Francisco Waldorf School for eight years. He was a founding parent at that school and has served on its Board for eighteen years. He is an artist and author, has published a book *Photography at Bay: Interviews, Essays, and Reviews*, and written extensively on aspects of Waldorf education and threefold organizational development.

Bill Bottum (now retired) was CEO of a construction company which did work throughout the U.S. and Saudi Arabia. He holds B.S.E. and M.S.E. degrees in Civil Engineering from the University of Michigan. He currently serves on the General Council of the Anthroposophical Society in America and on the boards of the R.K. Greenleaf Center* and the Rudolf Steiner Foundation.

Agaf Dancy earned his BA from Brandeis University and worked as a Computer Systems Analyst before becoming a Waldorf teacher. He studied at the Waldorf Institute in Southfield, Michigan before taking a class at the Rudolf Steiner School of Ann Arbor in 1982. During a sabbatical he earned an MA in Education from Eastern University and then took over two classes in the middle school. He went on to spearhead the development of the high school in Ann Arbor. He also founded and served as Board president for the Waldorf Teacher Development Association. In July 1998 Agaf and his family moved to Fair Oaks, California, to work as Administrative Coordinator for the Association of Waldorf Schools of North America.

Abraham Entin has been active in the anthroposophical movement since 1976. He has been a parent at Highland Hall Waldorf School since 1979 and has served on the Board of the Pasadena Waldorf School. He regularly consults for the Anthroposophical Society in America and is on the faculty of Rudolf Steiner College (Administrators' Course). He also consults with Waldorf schools on "How to Build Enrollment." Mr. Entin and his wife are the founders and owners of Diaperaps, Ltd., a natural diapering company founded in 1984. In addition, Mr. Entin has more than 35 years of professional marketing and market research experience. He hold degrees from the University of Chicago and UCLA.

Siegfried E. Finser, co-founder and Trustee of the Rudolf Steiner Foundation, has consulted with many government and non-profit institutions as well as many corporations in the United States and abroad. He was Treasurer of the Anthroposophical Society in America and President of the Threefold Educational Foundation. He managed a division of the Xerox Corporation and was Director of Human Resource Development for ITT with worldwide responsibility for the development of all executives. He has helped many Waldorf schools and other initiatives in an advisory capacity.

Lynn Kern is the Operations Manager of Highland Hall Waldorf School, where she serves on the Board of Directors and the College of Teachers. She is also the co-chair of DANA (the Development and Administrators' Network of AWSNA), and teaches at Rudolf Steiner College in the Administrator's Training Program. She previously served as the Vice-President of Credit and Public Affairs for a national department store with responsibility for sales exceeding $1 billion annually.

Dorothy Lenz is a minister emerita of the First Congregational Church in Ann Arbor, Michigan. She holds a B.A. degree in Journalism from the University of Minnesota and an M.A. degree in English from the University of Wyoming. For many years now she has had a special interest in the writings of Rudolf Steiner and Robert Greenleaf.*

David Mitchell is Chairman of AWSNA Publications and teaches life-science and architecture at Shining Mountain Waldorf High School. He has helped found three Waldorf elementary schools and one high school, and was part of the inauguration of the Antioch University M.Ed. program in New Hampshire. Throughout his twenty-eight years in Waldorf education he has been involved in administration—assuming such duties as faculty chairman, Board member, financial officer, and was for ten years Chairman of AWSNA's Eastern Region. Currently a member of the Western Regional Committee, he regularly consults with schools. He is the author and editor of many books on Waldorf education.

Dana Myers, CFRE, is the Director of Development at the Honolulu Waldorf School. She holds a Masters degree in Library Studies from the University of Hawaii. She is a Certified Fund Raising Executive of the National Society of Fund Raising Executives since 1995. Dana is currently a delegate to the Development and Administrative Network of AWSNA (D.A.N.A.) and a member of the AWSNA Development Committee. In addition to her work with Waldorf education, she is a fund raising and organizational consultant. She has extensive experience working with educational and cultural/artistic organizations. Ms. Myers is also the Managing Director for the Hawaii's Vocal Arts Ensemble, and serves on the Boards of the O'ahu Choral Society and the National Society of Fund Raising Executives-Aloha Chapter.

Martin L. Novom, CFRE, advises Waldorf schools and other nonprofit organizations on questions of philanthropy, governance, volunteerism, and administrative issues. He is a founding member, planner and presenter for Lemnis Conference Series, an experiential conference for non-pedagogical questions in the Pacific Northwest. He teaches at Sunbridge College, Rudolf Steiner College, Antioch New England, and the University of New Hampshire. He is also a presenter at conferences for fundraising professionals such as Continuing Education in Fundraising (NH) and National Society of Fundraising Exeuctives (NH, VT, ME). Martin is a certified fundraiser with the National Society of Fundraising Executives.

Cornelis Pieterse, MA. For over 12 years Cornelis has been an advisor to many Waldorf schools on questions of organization and social development. In that capacity, he facilitates visioning, planning and decision making processes, as well as collegial relationships. Cornelis was a founding member of the Chicago Waldorf School and a dormitory counselor/faculty member at High Mowing School. He has taught a variety of courses at Sunbridge, Antioch and Rudolf Steiner Colleges. Cornelis is a consultant with Lemnis Associates and a founding member of the Lemnis Conferences Series in the Pacific northwest. He received his Waldorf Teacher training from Emerson College (UK) and a MA in Marriage and Family Therapy from Antioch New England Graduate School, Keene, NH.

Lou Rossi entered the school movement as a parent in the Detroit Waldorf School in the early 70's. He joined the faculty at High Mowing School in 1976 and taught Physics and Chemistry until 1996. He studied under Hans Gebert at the Waldorf Teacher Training Institute in Detroit in 1974 - 76. At High Mowing he became Faculty Chair in 1983, a position he held until 1996 when he became Development Director and formed the school's first Development Office. In 1978 he joined a group of parents and friends to organize the school's Annual Giving drive and has been active in Development and Alumni Affairs since that time.

Christopher Schaefer, Ph.D., is a faculty member of Sunbridge College, and the Director of the Waldorf School Administration and Community Development Program. He is a Waldorf graduate, a former Waldorf parent and Board member, and has worked extensively with Waldorf schools in the U.S., Canada, and England on questions of organization and community renewal. He is the co-author of *Vision in Action: Working with Soul and Spirit in Small Organizations* (Lindisfarne) and the author of the forthcoming *Partnerships of Hope: Building Waldorf Schools and Other Communities of the Spirit.*

Robert Schiappacasse is the administrator at Shining Mountain Waldorf School in Boulder Colorado. He is a delegate to the Association of Waldorf Schools of North America (AWSNA), and the Rocky Mountain Regional Coordinator of the Development and Administrative Network of AWSNA (DANA) He teaches at Sunbridge College in Spring Valley, New York, and Rudolf Steiner College in Fair Oaks, California, in their Waldorf School Administration and Community Development programs. He lectures and consults with Waldorf schools on Waldorf school administration and community development.

Kay Skonieczny, Development Officer for AWSNA since October of 1996, started the development/public relations program at the Sacramento Waldorf School in 1979 and served the school in that capacity until 1986, when she left to became the Director of Fund Development for the Sacramento Girl Scout Council. Kay has consulted with churches, retreat centers and social service agencies, assisting them with fundraising campaigns and public relations programs.

Ann Stahl, director of Advisory Services of the Rudolf Steiner Foundation from its Spring Valley office, discovered Waldorf education in 1967 when looking for a kindergarten for her first child. At the time, she was teaching Early Childhood Education at an adult level after having taught in the public schools. Ann earned an MA in Early Childhood Education from Keene State University. Ann's daughter attended Green Meadow Waldorf School where Ann eventually became a kindergarten teacher. She began volunteer work with the Rudolf Steiner Foundation in 1984 and became a full time employee in 1985, first on the accounting side and then in advisory work, which she is still doing.

---

* In 1964, Greenleaf founded the Center for Applied Ethics. Renamed in 1985, The Greenleaf Center for Servant-Leadership, it is now an international, nonprofit, educational organization to encourage the understanding and practice of servant as leader by offering resources for study and development on three levels - personal, relational, and institutional (communal). If you are interested in further information, contact The Greenleaf Center for Servant-Leadership, 921 East Eighty-Sixth Street, Suite 200, Indianapolis, IN, 46240. Phone: (317) 259-1241